PRAISE FOR THE WISDOM OF

Extraordinary Putting

"Brilliant! I use Extraordinary Putting *principles in my golf lessons and in my life and they have made a profound difference. A must-read and reread for all the golfers looking to learn how to play this wonderful game. Fred has captured the joy of learning something new and made it simple. It will make a profound difference in how you look at yourself and how you learn this game. It is that important."*
—LAIRD SMALL, 2003 National PGA Teacher of the Year; a *Golf* magazine
  "Top 100 Teacher"; one of *Golf Digest*'s "50 Greatest Teachers in America"

"Fred Shoemaker's approach to the game allows us to discover the simple truth about whatever 'it' is that lets greatness flow on the putting green. The funny thing is that, while engaging in the process, you're also revealing the true 'you' that's been locked up for much too long, and becoming more attentive and freer in your personal and professional life."
—DEDRIC HOLMES, Senior Director of
  Life Skills Education, The First Tee

"For those who realize that golf is more than just a game, Extraordinary Putting *will be welcome reading, as it provides insights not just for golf, but for life."*
—STEVE CASE, cofounder of America Online and
  chairman of Revolution Health Group

"Growing up on the windswept links of Northern Ireland, you learn to play the game with feeling. Fred can explain and relate that better than anyone."
—DARREN CLARKE, European Tour player and Ryder Cup member

AND FOR

Extraordinary Golf

"I have never met a better teacher of golf's inner game. [Extraordinary Golf] *will become a classic."*
—MICHAEL MURPHY, author of *Golf in the Kingdom*

· Extraordinary ·
PUTTING

TRANSFORMING THE WHOLE GAME

FRED SHOEMAKER

with Jo Hardy

A Perigee Book

A PERIGEE BOOK
Published by the Penguin Group
Penguin Group (USA) Inc.
375 Hudson Street, New York, New York 10014, USA
Penguin Group (Canada), 90 Eglinton Avenue East, Suite 700, Toronto, Ontario M4P 2Y3, Canada
(a division of Pearson Penguin Canada Inc.)
Penguin Books Ltd., 80 Strand, London WC2R 0RL, England
Penguin Group Ireland, 25 St. Stephen's Green, Dublin 2, Ireland (a division of Penguin Books Ltd.)
Penguin Group (Australia), 250 Camberwell Road, Camberwell, Victoria 3124, Australia
(a division of Pearson Australia Group Pty. Ltd.)
Penguin Books India Pvt. Ltd., 11 Community Centre, Panchsheel Park, New Delhi—110 017, India
Penguin Group (NZ), Cnr. Airborne and Rosedale Roads, Albany, Auckland 1310, New Zealand
(a division of Pearson New Zealand Ltd.)
Penguin Books (South Africa) (Pty.) Ltd., 24 Sturdee Avenue, Rosebank, Johannesburg 2196, South Africa

Penguin Books Ltd., Registered Offices: 80 Strand, London WC2R 0RL, England

While the author has made every effort to provide accurate telephone numbers and Internet addresses at the time of publication, neither the publisher nor the author assumes any responsibility for errors, or for changes that occur after publication. Further, the publisher does not have any control over and does not assume any responsibility for author or third-party websites or their content.

PRINTING HISTORY
G. P. Putnam's Sons hardcover edition / April 2006
Perigee trade paperback edition / January 2007

Perigee trade paperback ISBN: 978-0-399-53308-2

The Library of Congress has cataloged the G. P. Putnam's Sons hardcover edition as follows:

Shoemaker, Fred.
    Extraordinary putting : Transforming the whole game / by Fred Shoemaker with Johanne Hardy.
      p. cm.
    ISBN 0-399-15333-0
    1. Putting (Golf)—Psychological aspects. I. Hardy, Johanne, date. II. Title.
  GV979.P8S46   2006   2005050948

PRINTED IN THE UNITED STATES OF AMERICA

10 9 8 7 6 5 4 3 2 1

Outdoor recreational activities are by their very nature potentially hazardous. All participants in such activities must assume the responsibility for their own actions and safety. If you have any health problems or medical conditions, consult with your physician before undertaking any outdoor activities. The information contained in this guide book cannot replace sound judgment and good decision making, which can help reduce risk exposure, nor does the scope of this book allow for disclosure of all the potential hazards and risks involved in such activities. Learn as much as possible about the outdoor recreational activities in which you participate, prepare for the unexpected, and be cautious. The reward will be a safer and more enjoyable experience.

I'D LIKE TO ACKNOWLEDGE . . .

My best friend, partner, wife and co-author, Jo Hardy, whose integrity, commitment, playful spirit and love have made this book, and so much more, possible.

My partner and coach, Garry Lester, whose insights and wisdom have shifted my life and influenced every page of this book.

Bill Condaxis and Evan Schiller, whose leadership, coaching and personal exploration have been an inspiration.

Marshall Gavre, Ed Hipp, John Allen, Tom Nordland and Michael Lach, whose deep commitment to coaching has "knocked 'em alive."

Steve McGee, Kim Larsen, Victor Whipp, Lisa Holzwarth, John Snopkowski and Chet Dunlop, who have contributed their life energy and shared their lives.

Gordon Starr and Robert Chester, whose deep trust in our work and pure delight in our achievements helped us move our vision from fantasy to real possibility.

Hilton Tudhope, whose keen intelligence and support have contributed to shaping this book.

Tim Gallwey, whose coaching principles opened up a rich, new dimension in learning.

Our community of Extraordinary Golf graduate students, whose courage and never-ending willingness to explore allowed the fullness of this material to come to life.

My family, who have always supported me. And especially my brother Pete, who once again helped organize this material and whose vision of a future that works for all has always provided sufficient oxygen to bring any spark that I may have to life.

Contents

EXTRAORDINARY
PUTTING

INTRODUCTION

I began giving golf lessons in the 1970s. Like most new teachers, I started out full of enthusiasm, intent on fostering great development in my students. Having been a top high school and college player, I was also full of enthusiasm about my own golf game, feeling that my best years were still ahead of me.

But after a few years the bloom began to fade from the rose, in both my coaching and my playing. Things were not working out the way I'd hoped. I needed a new perspective, and so arranged to meet with a well-known teacher to be coached on my teaching/coaching and on my own golf game. Although this man's expertise wasn't in golf, I thought he might have something significant to offer me. Little did I know how my life would change from his contribution.

He started our meeting with a question: "Would you like to have golf lessons be endlessly interesting or endlessly boring?" Of course I said, "Endlessly interesting!" Then he asked, "What's the truth about how it is for you right now?"

I looked back on the last few years. My first reaction was that giving golf lessons was great, but as I examined my experience more closely I realized the truth was that lessons were becoming pretty boring—that I was locked in a particular way of doing and saying the same things every day. Although I gave a lot of lessons and was financially successful, it just wasn't that interesting anymore, and I wasn't learning much. The same was true with my golf game.

After I told him this he said, "What would make it endlessly fascinating, endlessly interesting?" After some thought, I answered, "I don't know." "Well, maybe you want to consider finding out," he replied. "If you didn't have a purpose in golf before, you now have one: to find out how to create golf as an endless fascination. Because only then will you really learn. We only learn what we want to learn, what we're interested in learning, and learning is a function of fascination."

That meeting was more than twenty-five years ago. I took on his coaching that day—and every day since. The discoveries made from this exploration have transformed my lessons and my game. To this day both are completely fascinating.

This book is an attempt to share that fascination, and

the resultant learning, in one area of golf: putting. Even though this book is written in the first person, my "voice" is in essence the voice of my Extraordinary Golf coaching community, and the insights contained here are distilled from a vast body of collective experience.

Chapter One.

ANYTHING IS POSSIBLE

I'd arrived an hour and a half early for our Extraordinary Golf program, excited as usual. I wanted to set up the room for our students and get ready for our coaches' gathering.

One student had already arrived. He was planning to have breakfast before we began. On that particular day, the room didn't get set and he didn't have breakfast until an hour later. We had a conversation about things that were important to us, why we were there, what each of us intended for the next three days, etc.

Toward the end of the hour, he asked me what I had been up to lately. I said I'd just finished writing a book on putting. His reaction was different from what I had anticipated. Instead of saying, "That's great!" or "Way to go!" or "Who's your publisher?" he said, "Why putting? It's the minority in terms of shots, least ego-satisfying, least interesting in terms of practice, and considering all we've been talking about, I would have thought you would have chosen something with broader appeal, something on a grander scale."

I replied, "Because putting can open up the whole thing."

"You mean it can help your whole short game?"

I replied, "The whole thing."

"You mean your whole game?"

Again I replied, "The *whole thing*."

"I don't understand," he said.

I explained, "Would you consider the possibility that the way you are in putting is the way you are in chipping, is the way you are in your full swing, is the way you are with your family, in your business . . . the *whole thing*!"

"Come on! That's a big stretch!" he said. Then he paused and added, "I'll have to chew on that for a while."

I offered, "I understand that right now this notion is just a concept for you, but imagine if it were true that putting can both reveal and make a difference in the whole thing. Imagine that it can show us our relationship to learning, how our actions and behavior are shaped by our point of view, how we view and relate to our body, and how the depth of our awareness is the only thing that will develop us. Putting can show us the assumptions and beliefs that we have come to take for granted. It can reveal the interference—the doubt and fear that stop us everywhere in life. It can also show the genius of our body and provide a pathway to performance and enjoyment that we can take to any part of the game, or to any situation in life."

"I've been playing for twenty years and I've never gotten anything like that out of putting," he replied. "What I notice is simply, 'Did I make or miss?' and 'Am I putting well or not?' The things you're talking about seem to ask for something I'm unfamiliar with."

"Yes," I said. "The learning I'm talking about is an intentional act. It doesn't happen on its own. You have to create it. That may be what coaching is for—to bring out the type of learning that wouldn't happen in the normal course of events. That's what the putting book and the course we're about to start are all about. Extraordinary learning about the whole thing."

"Well," he said, "Let's get started!"

Yes, indeed, let's get started. . . .

.Chapter Two.

WHAT GOLFERS WANT

THE BOTTOM LINE

For something to become truly fascinating it must not only be interesting, it must also be relevant and meaningful. In other words, it must be something that gives you what you want. So the obvious question becomes, what do you want in golf? I mean, *really* want?

We've been asking that question of the thousands of people who've participated in our Extraordinary Golf programs over more than fifteen years. It's not an easy question to answer. From my experience, it's necessary to look beyond the first ready-made answer, the one that's about what our culture, with its emphasis on performance and achievement, says we should want. The truth is that this is a question the culture can't answer for you. It's one you have to answer for yourself and it may require some probing. In baseball oftentimes a manager will tell a hitter, "Take the first pitch. Let it go by. Don't swing at it." And so we've recommended that students do the same thing with their first responses to this question, which would typically be along the lines of "I want to be better. I want to be the best I can be," etc. Those responses are fine, but what's underneath them? "I want to be a better putter." Great. That can happen. But what's underneath that? What will that give you?

Another way of asking this question is, "Why do you play golf?" What's the point of it all? Why is the game worth playing for you? In *Extraordinary Golf* we've written down thousands of our students' responses to these questions. We've created programs to provide students with the environment to access what they want and honestly examine the question. What's emerged from a decade and a half of exploration is something fascinating and not so predictable. It's also the basis of this book. What golfers of all ages—both men and women, from tour professionals to beginners—are looking for is dominated by three primary desires. Their requests indicate that the source of extraordinary performance, great enjoyment and high learning is not that complex.

The three things most requested by golfers are the following:

Freedom
Peace of mind
Increased awareness and the ability to self-coach

Of course, along the way students have also asked for the things you might expect: solid mechanics, a smooth stroke, a good grip, alignment, concentration, to play/putt well under pressure and to learn to read greens. But what's the source of these technical developments? What's the cause that produces the effects? After fifteen years of listening to our students' requests and seeing the outcomes, I have seen that the source of great putting development (and all of golf development) is exactly what students say they want: freedom, peace of mind and increased awareness. Therefore this book is divided into three sections, with exercises focused on the development of these qualities. Here's the basic promise and premise:

The exercises don't work. *You* do.

Consider the possibility that you may be far more able than you think and that when you let go of self-interference and increase your awareness, you will see exceptional ability emerge. The following exercises are opportunities for experiences that may show you how extraordinary and capable you already are.

Chapter Three

THE CONTEXT

FROM DEPENDENCY TO SELF-RELIANCE

Several friends of mine work for private international relief organizations committed to solving the issues of chronic hunger and starvation in underdeveloped countries. They tell me that from 1975 to 1995 they thought the source of chronic hunger to be simply the absence of food. At times of crisis during that time period, the organizations responded by bringing in large amounts of food aid into Ethiopia, Uganda, Biafra, Somalia, Bangladesh and India, among others.

But the more time they spent with people who live in hunger, and with the people who work to feed them, the more they came to see the source of chronic hunger as something much more than the absence of food. My friend Lynne Twist captures the scope of the problem in her book *The Soul of Money:*

> The societal effect of massive aid of this kind was that people at the receiving end became more disabled and more impoverished than they were before. They felt debilitated and helpless by the fact they couldn't take care of themselves and had become welfare recipients, beholden to outsiders to bail them out again and again. They felt lessened and weakened and the future prospect of their own self-sufficiency was often suppressed and diminished by the behavior they needed to exhibit to get their hands on "free food."

The net effect from massive amounts of donated aid, in every country, was that the people of those countries saw themselves—and were seen by relief workers—as less capable, less self-reliant and less sufficient. Despite the best of intentions, the organizations had fostered dependency and had not improved the long-term condition of the people in the country. Recognizing the need for a fundamental shift in their approach, several organizations set about reinventing the concept of aid and started investing in the transformation of the status quo, rather than in its continuation.

Aid workers reconceived their role to that of listening, enlivening and *empowering* host country men and women to, in turn, create their own vision, unite their communities and form their own work teams. Relief organizations learned to create partnerships of empowerment—not dependency—in which people mobilize themselves for self-reliant action. Aid now comes in the form of micro-credit and seed money to jump-start visions, supporting communities to create their own plans, move into action and find out how capable they are and always were. The results have been astounding, and they continue to grow.

THE TIP VS. THE EXPERIENCE

So what does this have to do with a book about putting? Let me make the transition for you.

Our primary medium of exchange in the field of golf teaching has been predominantly one thing: the tip. A tip is a statement of what to do, usually given by the teacher to the student. "Take the club back straight." "Keep the clubface square." "Follow through to the target." "Stay relaxed." "Stay down." You know them. They are everywhere and they are the way that most golf is taught in this country. Ironically, it's believed that the reason golfers don't develop—why there is "chronic hunger" for golf improvement—is the absence of tips and information. The editor of a major golf magazine said, "If we put the word 'tip' on the cover, the sales always jump. It's what readers look for and expect."

In a sense, a tip is a donation from someone who "knows more," someone self-reliant, to someone perceived as less so, in the hope that the recipient will take the tip and grow, much like a donation to an underdeveloped country.

In the beginning, these tips may seem like they make a difference. If you tell someone they're lined up to the right, they then line up to the left. But have you ever watched them in the long run? When the tip giver is no longer standing behind the tip recipient? Rarely does the alignment remain accurate over time. And even more rarely does the student's trust grow.

It seems as though most people in golf are waiting for a tip to make them better. And if there are conclusions I've come to after seeing this form of coaching for the last thirty years, it is that tips foster dependency and interfere with the individual's ability to really grow. Students never learn to trust themselves and to develop their full capability. Tips are disabling, not empowering. They do not lead to self-sufficiency and they ultimately sabotage self-coaching.

Just as the people in the underdeveloped countries grew to become self-directed and self-reliant, it's possible for golfers to become self-coaching—able to guide their own development.

ESSENTIAL LEARNING

So what is self-coaching and why is it important? At the fundamental level, self-coaching involves learning, so a more basic question would be, what is learning? And how do you know when you've learned something?

Let's start with a simple example that's familiar to all of us. As a youngster I learned addition, and now, somehow, when I am asked to add 4 and 4, I know that the sum is 8. I also learned that the moon has one-sixth the gravity of the earth. Is this a kind of learning? Well, it is certainly an increase in understanding, and most people will view that as positive. I can certainly provide the appropriate answers on a test, and when I look at the moon, for example, I can re-call that gravitational fact. This type of learning is intricately connected with the term "knowledge." I have learned and I have knowledge. This acquisition of knowledge is a familiar process, but in the context of this book there is a more im-portant question: Is this kind of learning valuable for golf?

Let's take a look at this in golf by using a full swing exam-ple. Let's say that you know you swing outside in, across the ball with an open clubface, and you "know" this because of the following: your ball starts out to the left and slices back (this comes from the laws of ball flight, which you have memorized); your friends and your pro have told you that your clubface is open; you've seen your divots point to the left with the right side of the divot cut in like a small trench; and you've seen it on video. Because of this information, you feel you know that you swing outside in with an open clubface.

My experience as a player and teacher has shown me that none of this results in actual *knowing,* at least not the kind that makes a difference in golf. I would relabel them as beliefs and conceptual understanding, and I have never seen them lead to the type of self-coaching and self-reliance from which amazing performance comes. This is still the type of knowing that comes from information and tips.

In golf, the value of knowledge is determined by the *way* something is known—not simply by *what* we know but *how* we know it. Another way of knowing something, and a way that creates self-coaching, is called *experiential* know-ing. I'll use another word for it later ("distinguishing") but for now I will call it experiential.

When people come to Extraordinary Golf, it's pretty obvious most of them "know" their putting stroke and their full swing through concepts and beliefs. But given the limitations of concepts and beliefs, few can coach themselves well. So we create an environment where students are exposed to the experience itself, in the moment it occurs, in action. People ask me whether this means "feeling." It certainly includes feeling and all the senses, but it encompasses much more than that. It resonates on many different levels. It is an "aha" experience.

When we watch students experience things for the first time, we watch their lightbulbs go on. We hear comments such as, "I *know* it now. I know where my club is. I know where the clubface is!" This is the beginning of true self-coaching, and I've never seen it come from understanding or information. This kind of self-coaching translates into immediate growth in performance. Instead of having the same thoughts, imitating past experiences and living in the same beliefs and concepts, students are having direct, original experiences of things they've never experienced before, and it's very powerful.

In Extraordinary Golf, we promise students an environment without judgment or evaluation in which it is possible for them to have direct experiences that allow them to become self-coaching. For them, and for all golfers, the type of knowledge that comes from experiencing our swing or putting stroke is something we can't get from anyone else. We can only get it from ourselves. When we have this kind of knowing, then understanding, beliefs and concepts are irrelevant.

So we have a clear juxtaposition of two paths to development: the tip versus the experience. The first produces, at best, very slow development; the second a more rapid and self-reliant development.

So what is the access to direct experiences? Your awareness. The experience of freedom, peace of mind and self-coaching that can transform your golf will come only from expanding your awareness, which is the simple act of being present to something as it is happening in the moment.

Part One

FREEDOM
EXPLORATIONS

THE STARTING POINT

At a certain point in our Extraordinary Golf program, we gather people on the putting green and invite them to examine their putting game. One of the coaches asks, "In order to maximize performance, learning and enjoyment, what is the very first thing you need to know?"

People consider the question for a while and usually come up with answers that are about their goals, the method of achieving them, their resources, etc. The coach then says, "That's actually part of what you would need to know in the *second* phase. What's the first? Another way of asking is, 'If you were traveling by car to a city, say New York, what is the first thing you would need to know?'"

STUDENT: A map, a route to get there?
COACH: What would you need to know even *before* that?
STUDENT (*after some time and consideration*): I would need to know where I am right now, what my starting point is!

Isn't the first question that must be asked in exploring excellence in performance, "What's the truth about where I am right now?" Yet almost no one goes there first. Knowing where you are is just as crucial in developing your skills as it is in navigating to a destination, and if you recognize this you've got a huge amount of development already under way.

Once students agree that this is the starting point, we invite them to apply it to putting. We ask them to putt and discover where they are right now and report back in ten minutes. This is very difficult to do because it requires them to step back and observe themselves—their process—while they're in it. It's asking them what key swing thoughts run through their heads, what pieces of advice they give themselves, what assumptions they have about how things should be, what things they think they must remember, and how and when they judge their putts. It's asking them to look at the internal context in which they putt as well as the mechanical stuff that fills their heads. It's a bit like going to the movies and watching yourself watch the movie, and it can be tricky. But this is essential to understanding "where I am right now—where I am when I putt."

It's amazing what students come back with as they begin

to observe themselves. Here's a small sampling of what they tell themselves:

> Stay still.
> Keep your eyes over the ball.
> Relax your arms.
> Make a forward swing equal to the backswing.
> Back of the left hand to target.
> Accelerate.
> Don't peek.
> Move only your arms and shoulders.
> I can make it.
> I can't make it.
> Soft grip.
> Just get it close.
> Let the putter swing.

And on and on . . .

There are hundreds of things that go through their heads! Each person seems to have a particular list of "stuff" to remember—a series of tips and techniques that they believe is crucial to their being able to putt well. This is a real eye-opener for students, as they start to see how much they've put on top of what is essentially the very simple action of rolling a ball toward a hole. We encourage them to recognize and voice as much as they can. They soon see that there's so much that it's nearly impossible to get everything out.

When the self-observation process is as complete as it can be, a coach might say, "So where are you when you putt?" The question is usually met with puzzled looks:

"What do you mean where am I? I'm right here on the green!" The coach replies, "I can see that. And while you were putting, where were you? What part of your anatomy were you in?" This is usually met by silence as the students consider what to them is a very unusual question. But after a while, the answer becomes obvious. "I'm in my head!" someone will say. "I'm thinking, hoping, judging, fearing and remembering. I'm in some mental process."

Once this realization comes before the group it's like a lightbulb going on, and everyone sees the truth of it for him- or herself. If you look at the list of instructions students give themselves, you'll see that "I'm in my head" is true for just about all golfers. We're constantly "talking" to ourselves over our putts ("Stay still."). We're remembering formulas ("Move only my arms and shoulders."). We're thinking either negatively or positively ("I can't make it." "I can make it."). We're in our heads most of the time.

After realizing this, students often say, "Where else *can* I be?" The coach then makes a simple request: "Would you be willing to explore a new possibility? Not that it's the right one, but now that you can see what it is you have, you have a choice: to stay with what you have, or to open up to a new possibility. I'm asking you if you would be willing to let go of your way for a little while so that we can explore some new ways of looking at things."

As the saying goes, "In order to explore new lands, you have to leave the one you're in." As we know with famous explorers like Magellan, such journeys take a lot of courage, and this is true even in golf. It's not easy to let go of familiar ways of doing things, but without doing so you have no room for anything new. Are you ready?

• *The "Where Are You Now?" Exercise* •

Putt for ten minutes in your normal way, simply observing what you do. Pay particular attention to the following:

- What you tell yourself as you address the putt.
- What tips you think you need to remember.
- When do judgments arise: before, during or after the putt?

The clearer you can see the foundation on which you have built your putting—the assumptions, stories, things to remember, judgments, evaluations, etc.—the more clearly and powerfully you can explore the rest of the exercises.

Chapter Four.

Freedom Exploration #1: The Spot

Okay, let's get a little weird right off the bat. If you can handle this exercise, you can handle any of them. Continuing with our earlier scenario of working with students in our Extraordinary Golf programs . . .

We gather the group together and ask everyone to place a ball on the ground in front of them and kneel down to look at it. We ask the students what they see. I know this may seem like an odd question, but we point out to them that they've been looking at golf balls through all their years of play and we'd like to know what they really see. People say lots of things: the brand name, the number, the dimples, etc. We ask them to keep looking for what they've never seen before. Perhaps they've never noticed that on any given day some of the dimples are in the shade, some in sunlight and some are half-and-half like the craters on the moon. Not many of them have. We also point out that the sun creates a sheen on top of the ball even on a cloudy day, and that there's sunlight reflecting in some of the dimples. If you ask how many people have ever noticed the sun reflecting on the dimples, usually about one in ten has. We then ask them to do something they've probably never done before, as described below.

• *Freedom Exploration Exercise #1a* •
The Spot

(a) Place a golf ball on the ground. Kneel down and take some time to look at it and really see it. *Look for the shading, the overall light and the sparkles. Look for what you haven't seen before.*

(b) Keep looking at the ball for a few moments. Then, without covering the top of the ball with your hand, reach along the ground, hold the ball on the sides with finger and thumb and gently pull it away to the side while keeping your eyes on the spot where the ball was. *As you look at the area where the ball was, what do you see? If you don't see anything, do it again. Take your time. Make sure you do not follow the ball with your eyes, but keep staring at the spot on the ground where the ball was.*

If you're really staring at the whiteness of the golf ball, and the ball is pulled away, you're looking at the grass below it and you will see a spot on the ground, in the same way you would see a spot if you looked at a lightbulb and turned

LOOKING AT THE BALL

SEEING THE SPOT

away and looked at a wall. It's called a retinal after-image, and we refer to it as simply the "after-image." Almost every time you get a group of people to experience seeing it, they say "Wow!" and laugh because they've usually never noticed it before. Very few people have. Students often ask the coaches, "How did you come to see that?" Maybe a more relevant question is to ask the students, "Where have you been that you've never seen that?" Because this after-image can be seen *every single time* you hit a golf ball (not just in putting but in all shots), and for some of you that may be as many as a million balls. Where have you been that you've not seen it? It reinforces the fact that when most golfers hit a ball they are "not there." They are in some mental process rather than being present to the physical reality in which golf is played.

• *Freedom Exploration Exercise #1b* •
The Spot While Putting

Address a ball in your normal putting stance and, as before, look at the ball for a few seconds to let it fill your vision. Then putt the ball to no target and watch for the after-image on the ground. See how long the spot lasts. Do this for ten minutes or so.

After fifteen years of doing this exercise with students (many of whom are golf professionals), I have heard, without fail, astounding reports. People speak of a calmness of mind, a sense of freedom and ease, a lack of worry and the disappearance of the mental checklist. It's an amazing experience and very powerful, and the reason is quite simple: For most students, seeing the spot is the first time they've experienced being truly present in golf—the first time they've been able "to be there" while putting, rather than being entangled in remembering some tip or making an evaluation about how they're doing. For the first time, they've made their way out of a mental activity (thoughts about what to do or how they did) to a state of awareness.

BEING HERE NOW

We've all heard of concepts such as "being present" or "in the now," as they have become more and more a part of public discourse and have made their way into a great number of books and articles. The beauty of golf is that it can help bring such deep concepts to life and give us a simple and very effective way to experience them. The "seeing the spot" exercise illuminates a profound truth about our inner world.

There are three places we can have our attention in life:

1. the future, a state wherein we're thinking about what might happen at some upcoming point in time;
2. the past, a state of recall where we're thinking about what has happened; and
3. the present, simply being here, aware of what is happening now.

Most golfers typically approach a shot trying to remember what they should do (based on what they've done in the past), and then they go into a mode of anticipating or hoping about the future. Thus they are never actually in the present moment, and this is true for most of us.

When we're truly present, putting becomes physical. We experience the environment through our senses instead of thinking about it. It's the difference between falling in love and reading a romance novel.

Contrast your experience at the beginning of this exploration (the "Where Are You Now?" exercise) to the experience of seeing the spot. Almost everyone has said that the two are completely different, but see for yourself.

Seeing the spot demands that you be in the present moment. In fact, it will be nearly impossible for you to see it if you're engaged in mental activity. This simple exercise is a feedback mechanism of your capacity to be present because the spot will likely last as long as you stay present. As soon as you start thinking, remembering, anticipating, hoping, wishing, evaluating, judging, assessing—making it a mental process—the spot will likely disappear.

People report that the after-image lasts anywhere from one to twenty seconds. They describe the experience of being fully present as very joyful, and they notice that time seems to stop. Their mental chatter subsides and they feel calmer. They often reflect on the fact that their greatest joy in life is being present in a similar way.

So how do you stop the craziness, the busyness in your head on the course? One way is by being fascinated in the present. Since this sport requires us to look at this small white sphere, why not create a fascination with it?

The great fundamentals of putting are a calm mind, an even stroke, a steady body and a solid hit. What's interesting about this little exercise is that 80 percent of our students report that they hit the ball more solidly when they're engaged in watching for the after-image. Most say their stroke evened out on its own, without any work. When asked if their body and head were steady throughout this exercise, almost every student says yes. And, when asked how many found they had less mental activity when being present in this way—less thinking and remembering—everyone reports that they did. In essence, all the fundamentals emerge.

LEARNED BUT NOT TAUGHT

As a coach, it was a shock to realize that although the fundamentals of golf have to be *learned,* they don't have to be *taught.* When one is present to some reality, such as the ball, the fundamentals start to show up—in all people. This remarkable occurrence highlights one of the biggest differences I see between teaching and coaching. Teaching assumes that something is missing in the student and the teacher has to provide it. Coaching assumes that the student's ability is already there, and only needs to be discovered and brought out.

Having watched people do this exercise for many years, I continue to be awed by how much inherent ability people have. It's amazing how putting strokes begin to change and shift, with people reporting back that it's almost too simple. The state of being fully present, and the awareness that it automatically brings, causes an almost magical transformation.

But again, don't just take my word for it—experience it for yourself. When one can stay present for putting, amazing things start to show up. In fact, it's the only time that amazing things start to show up. We're just not used to trusting and allowing the seeming lack of control that this exercise requires. We're also not used to being present, either in golf or in the rest of our lives, even though being present is essential to learning and performance. More important, we don't *know* we're not present. We don't notice that we've drifted away from the present moment to some thought about the past (an instruction, a memory, etc.) or to the future (the anticipation of a result).

NO FUTURE, NO PAST

Let me digress a bit. I promise to come back to golf and show you the relevance of my comments.

Another way of looking at the situation is to ask the question "When is the future?" If you really examine it, there really is no such thing as "the future." The future, as mentioned a few pages back, is something you're making up in an internal conversation with yourself *right now.* It's a thought you're having *now* about some time other than this time.

And when is the past? This is also a thought you are having about some other time, a thought that you are having *right now.* There are no such things as the future and the past. You can't go there. They are creations, concepts, and the only time you can create them is right now.

The present is what's happening outside of those thoughts. It *is* right now. In actuality, everything is happening now—past, present and future.

Two out of the three happen inside our heads (future and past), and one happens in reality. When you're in an internal conversation about the future, you're never in this moment, this reality. When you're in a conversation about the past, you're not in this moment either. Being in reality—this moment—is where learning takes place, where performance is effortless and enjoyment is natural. And it's amazing how little time we actually spend in this moment. So these exercises are about being right here, right now and experiencing what the present gives you. I discuss how the future has an impact on the present at the end of this book as well.

Back to golf . . . Let's return to the after-image of the ball and now add a target.

• *Freedom Exploration Exercise #1c* • *The Spot to a Target*

Address a ball in your normal putting stance and, as before, look at the ball for a few moments to let it fill your vision. Then putt the ball to a hole and watch for the after-image on the ground. See how long the spot lasts. Do this for ten minutes or so.

Does the addition of the hole change your experience? It's important to see whether it does and how. Notice whether you can be present to the after-image for the duration you intend or whether the target takes you away into some future projection, some evaluation. Now that you're putting to a target, are you thinking about results rather than simply being aware of the spot? Does the result—the future—cloud the present, your ability to be with the ball? If so, what kind of courage and intention would it take to actually be in this moment right here, no matter what, even when you have a target?

The internal chatter may momentarily get louder. The theme of it may be "You won't be able to get the ball close to the hole because you're not remembering things you need to remember." That's the sort of thing that will pop into your head, but the goal of this exercise is simple: Can you be present for the duration of the after-image even though there's a target? Notice the moments when you get pulled away. Where did you go? To the outcome? To remembering something? Being able to catch yourself when you go away is as powerful for learning as knowing that you stay present. Noticing that you go away gives you the possibility of coming back.

People report amazing things from focusing on the spot while putting to a target. Some say that when they can fully be with the ball, they also begin to have an experience of the target—*without trying.* Some say that for the first time they begin to get a sense of the club in their hands, the putter. These insights hint at another premise: When you can really be there for one thing, you can begin to have it all. When you can be with the spot fully, your awareness of the ball expands to include other things. But if you can't be there with one thing, nothing else will begin to show up.

If putting to a target diminishes your capacity to be present to the ball's after-image, you can safely assume that all the training you've been doing up to this point has been about anticipation of results (the future). You've essentially trained yourself away from the present moment into some other moment, and your training is showing up. But it's possible to retrain yourself and develop the capacity to be fully present to the ball while putting to a target. You can train yourself to come back to this moment, right now, once you've seen yourself being taken away.

Of course your mind will come up with all sorts of questions: "If I'm just present to the ball, how will I know how hard to hit it? How will I know where the target is?" Can you let those be for now and just come back to the after-image?

These "see the spot" exercises are about being present to a reality (a ball is real) rather than to a story in your head. They're about letting go of interference, the mental chatter that pervades and controls so much of our lives. Through these exercises you get an opportunity to see how good your body really is. You may never know until you start being present.

Chapter Five

FREEDOM EXPLORATION #2:
PUTTING TO
THE FLAGSTICK

I n one way, golf is inherently meaningless. By itself, hitting a piece of rubber into a hole 400 yards away does nothing valuable for society—literally nothing. If all the golfers in my town were to reduce their number of strokes per round, it wouldn't make one bit of difference in the town. Even on an individual basis, if people lower their handicaps it doesn't do anything for them that's really important. By itself, it doesn't increase their bank accounts (other than for touring professionals), doesn't make them better citizens and doesn't develop their relationships. If the point of golf is only about being good at golf, then much of the value that the game can provide gets missed.

The purpose of the game must be, at some level, to add

richness to life. That richness can be brought out through the following inquiry: "Is there anything important in this game that I would like to learn? Can I use the make-believe circumstances in this game to somehow enhance my life?"

So the most important question becomes what can we learn while we're learning to play golf? From my experience, quite a lot. We can learn about trust, freedom, handling difficult situations, overcoming obstacles and calming the disruptive voice in our head. We can learn about handling fear, self-doubt and frustration. We can learn how to learn. The list goes on and on, and this raises the possibility that the highest purpose of the game might be to learn about something other than the game.

But almost everything I've been talking about is thrown out the window when we watch golf on television or read about it in newspapers and sports magazines. The predominant view in the media is that golf itself has huge importance. Endless stories are told about what a win would mean to the rookie, the veteran or the person who has never won the "big one," and how this would affect their "place in history." Millions of words are written about "pressure" and how some people "have what it takes." Hence, a fantasy is created to get people to believe that rolling a ball into a hole is truly meaningful and that they should pay great attention to how others do it by of course reading the papers and watching television.

Every advertiser knows that it's important to associate some value or meaning with a product in order for the advertisement to have a strong impact: Buy this driver and people will respect you for the power you'll exhibit; drive this car and you'll have freedom and fulfillment. We're exposed to such a constant stream of media messages that we slip into accepting these associations between products and values without realizing we've done so, without challenging them. In golf, we've come to believe that if we score poorly it says something negative about us, and that if we score well, amazing things will happen to us. We think that the way we swing a golf club says a lot about who we are: that we are a better person if we hit the ball straight; that we have more character when we make a putt than when we miss it.

The stories created on how we play and what it means about us would be fine if they were seen as fantasies, but they are not seen that way. They are often seen as real, and they are the source of a great deal of interference. It's very difficult not to get caught up in the stories and project them onto our lives. This belief ("I am my performance") can be so strong that people can get upset when someone tries to poke fun at it.

Because many golf teachers and coaches have also bought into this myth, most of our golf experience is dominated by these stories, and they are a major source of interference when we play. We live out an existential drama while standing over a putt, searching for "meaning." We're so much at the effect of the meaning that we may not actually experience the putt, our body, the club and the target. We experience the drama.

I am not saying that this applies to just some of us, I'm saying that it applies to all of us. I've never met a person in all my forty thousand golf lessons who had completely separated their sense of self from their performance. Consequently, we have a great deal of interference, and this interference causes overtightening of muscles and lack of freedom. The outcome is that we don't putt nearly as well as we could.

Every exercise so far has been designed to get you back to who you are and help you let go of the unwanted drama. Let's continue.

• *Freedom Exploration Exercise #2a* •
The Flagstick

Take the flagstick out of the hole and lay it about 6 inches to the side of the hole, extending left to right. (If you do not have a flagstick available use a long golf club, such as a driver.) Stand about 6 feet away and putt at the flagstick stretched out on the green before you. Just putt with the purpose of hitting the stick. It doesn't matter where on the stick the ball hits. Putt a dozen balls and experience what your muscles feel like, where your attention is, how calm your mind is.

PUTTING TO A FLAGPOLE OR GOLF CLUB

You simply putt at the flag, trying to hit the pole from 6 feet away. Anyone can do it. It's so easy it probably seems silly. But because it's so easy there's no mental drama going on. When you take away the story about what putting means and how difficult and intricate it is, it's amazing how putting strokes become much more free and relaxed. Notice how much freedom is in your stroke. Notice how consistently and squarely you hit the ball. The action of hitting the ball—the reality of putting—is the same as with any putt under any conditions; the only thing missing is the internal melodrama that gets in the way.

Of course the next step, as I'm sure you're beginning to realize, is to change the target and notice the difference.

• *Freedom Exploration Exercise #2b* • *The Flagstick and the Target*

Now turn and putt the ball to the hole—which should be about the same distance as the flagstick—and notice if anything is different. Pay attention to the tightness of your muscles, the freedom of your movement and the thoughts in your head. Go back and forth between putting to the hole and putting to the flagstick to highlight any differences.

Remember, the game is about becoming aware of what's going on with you and noticing how you change when putting to the two different targets, not about how many times you get the ball in the hole. Because your success is assured when putting to the flagstick there will be less self-imposed "pressure" (internal drama), so this motion will be much closer to your natural stroke. Putting to the hole will likely bring up a host of stories and assumptions. What's it like to experience something that you might call "difficult" in contrast to experiencing what you can't miss? Both are merely experiences in the mind. In reality, it's just putting. The game is to notice the difference that the stories make.

CLIFF NOTES

This exercise has its origin some years ago when I would occasionally go to the top of a cliff overlooking a deep valley. I would tee up some balls and hit them with my driver into the valley. It didn't matter where they landed (there was no concern about hitting anyone)—I just enjoyed seeing them fly. I noticed that I hit the ball solidly with the same distance, flight and curve with stunning consistency. My experience of the swing was that it was simple and effortless. It dawned on me that the removal of the story about the possibility of failure—I couldn't miss the valley—lessened a great deal of interference, and that what remained was the free swing that was already there. I started to become aware of how I interfere with this swing on the golf course, so the game began to be to notice that interference. I eventually found that a simple way to do this in putting is to notice if I was different when putting at a flagstick on the ground versus putting at the hole.

On the golf course, whatever has our mind has our body—whatever has our attention has an effect on our body. The first thing to realize is that if our mind is concerned with difficulty or meaning (something at stake), our body will tighten up. When I was on the cliff top, the story about doubt and difficulty fell away. What showed up was me, the real me. This awareness began to bolster my trust in my innate ability, in who I really am when the layers of self-interference are removed. When I went to a golf course, I began to realize that my swing wasn't the problem. The problem was how I interfered with my natural ability. After a while I realized that this interference was due to some particular narrative I was engaged in, usually something along the lines of how much this shot meant.

Over the years I've closed a great deal of the gap between who I am on the cliff top and who I am on the golf course. The awareness that mishits on the course are due not to a lack of technique but rather to interference and a lack of freedom was a breakthrough. Through this insight I was able to give my full attention to the reality of what I was doing, and give up the perpetual conversation that my mechanics were just not good enough.

So begin to notice whether the freedom that you have while putting to the hole is the same as what you have while putting to the flag. What does your mind say about the putt and how important or difficult it is? What meaning are you giving it? This kind of mental stream isn't there when a five-year-old putts toward a hole. It's likely that a child is experiencing something like you experience when putting to the flagstick. One of the differences between kids and adults is that adults have a greater capacity to interfere. Without recognizing it, we're engaged in stories while we're standing over a putt, and these stories are a major cause of self-interference.

All the freedom exercises are designed to get you back to

your natural ability and show you how remarkable you are. They're designed to help you realize that you don't need to be more than you are, or different. Try looking at it this way: It's the interference that makes you different, and when you let go of it you come back to being yourself. It's a nice place to get back to.

Chapter Six

FREEDOM EXPLORATION #3: CONNECTING TO A TARGET

STEP ONE: ADDING NUMBERS

Each person has a putting stroke that is uniquely his or hers. It's the stroke that emerges when they stop manipulating their motion. While producing such a stroke may sound easy, it's actually quite difficult for most people because the manipulation has become transparent, unseen. So how do you strip away all the layers and get down to your natural stroke? And if you could, would you even want to? When I first talk to people about rediscovering their natural motion, most think it's not a good idea. Operating from the fundamental belief that they are not fully capable and that "something's missing" in themselves and in their swing, they assume that their natural motion is flawed and that even if they found it they'd want something else. They feel they must become better than they are because fundamentally they think they're not very good.

This is a complete lie. The problem is not lack of ability but interference with ability. This interference has a great deal to do with not being present, as most golfers putt while remembering or recalling something on every single stroke. If you accept the premise that you're really not good enough, of course you'd want to do something other than what you naturally do. I'm going to challenge this premise because what is underneath all the layers of remembering, trying and hoping is your real motion, the one you can repeat and the one that provides consistency. This motion may be the only thing you can trust on the greens, in timing and technique. It's natural to who you are. The golfers who play closest to their natural motion improve the fastest, experience the least stress and generally enjoy a much more satisfying game.

Here's what we do during our Extraordinary Golf programs to get to the heart of this issue. We ask a volunteer the question: "Can you add simple numbers?" People can get a little nervous at this question so we reassure them that the point of the exercise is not to test their math abilities but to determine whether they feel comfortable adding simple numbers from 1 to 5. They usually say yes so we ask them to add a few and not say anything until they have the answer. For instance, I might say (at a moderate pace), "Two. One. Two." They answer, "Five." I say (again, pacing it moderately), "Three, two, two." They say, "Seven." Then I use the fingers of one hand to display the numbers in sequence rather than speak them. For instance, I hold up two fingers, then three, then one. The person replies, "Six." I ask if it was difficult to pay attention to the numbers when I use my fingers, and most people say no. Then I walk to a spot just beyond a golf hole and use my hand to show another sequence of numbers from the back of the cup, and they respond in the same way as before.

Once we've established this part of the exercise, we move to the next, which involves a partner.

• *Freedom Exploration Exercise #3a* • *Adding Numbers*

Address a ball about 4 feet from a hole. Have a partner crouch behind the hole, facing you. When you are ready to putt, turn your head to look at the hole, say "go" and putt, looking only at the hole. As soon as you say "go," your partner displays

ADDING NUMBERS

three numbers (from 1 to 5) at an even pace at the back of the hole. Add the numbers while putting and say the total. Once you turn your head and say "go," do not look back at the ball.

Students typically respond, "You want me to add numbers while I'm putting?!" Yes, that's the exercise. "While I'm looking at the hole, not at the ball?" Yes. Line up, turn your head to the hole, and when you're ready to putt say "go" and putt. Don't wait for the numbers—just putt. Your partner will give you the numbers to add after you say go.

The job of the person putting is to give 100 percent of their attention to adding the numbers, not to getting the ball to the hole. Adding numbers is their *entire* job. The partner's job is simply to provide numbers (simple digits between 1 and 5) with one hand at the back of the cup.

In the beginning, almost everyone who does this exercise tries to remember something such as a key swing thought, or they look back at the ball just before they putt. Or they might see the numbers but not be able to add them, or not even see them at all. This is all fine, and expected. After a short time, however, most people get the idea to simply add the numbers and let go of any other interfering thoughts. Again, this exercise is about adding the numbers, not worrying about getting the ball in the hole. After they putt I ask the students whether or not they gave all their attention to the numbers. If they didn't, I stay with the exercise as long as it takes for them to fully be with the numbers. And their putting? It simply happens.

Filming this exercise is stunning. At some point—you can see it in the videos—people just let go and putting takes place while they're adding numbers. They don't understand how they can possibly be putting effectively because they're no longer remembering all that they thought they needed to remember in order to putt. But putting happens. It becomes an act of trust, and the most interesting part is that while the mind is occupied, the body learns how to putt.

This exercise accomplishes two things: First, it focuses the mind on an area that has some value, i.e., the back of the hole—the target. Second, it occupies the mind and keeps it from interfering with your putting stroke.

PURPOSEFUL DISTRACTION

I've never been one for distraction simply for its own sake. However, in the beginning it's not a bad idea to distract the mind because when this happens amazing things start to occur. If the putter happens to be pointed a little right or a little left, the putts will miss in the beginning, and they will miss on the same side, the same way. It's a wonderful clue to the source of consistency. Consistency happens when you stop doing all the extraneous stuff you're doing. When the mind is occupied by adding numbers, what comes out is an unadulterated, consistent putting stroke. If the putter happens to be pointing toward the hole, it's amazing how many go in.

So what's the point? If the ball can still go in the hole without remembering all the putting tips, what does this say about all the other stuff you were trying to do? If performance can happen without the checklist, without all the tips and techniques, then what's the point of all that stuff? What is it like to fully let go of our precious control and just putt? It's intentional without caring. It's focused without trying. These are very difficult states to achieve for most people, but they can be achieved, and the first thing is to realize that they are possible. It's possible that when you simply let go and trust your body's wisdom, putting can occur in a more effective way than ever before. Maybe what's already there—the putting technique that happens when you stop trying—is enough, or even more than enough. And maybe your idea of control has nothing to do with efficiency. Most people know that on some level letting go of control yields real control, but how many people are able to practice it?

In almost every case of working with students in this exercise, fascinating things occur. The students' putting strokes change when they start really letting go of *trying* to putt and start surrendering to just adding the numbers. Natural acceleration—the opposite of the jerky motion seen in most cases—also begins to appear. There's no guiding or steering the ball to the hole and rarely does anyone leave a putt short. One of the purposes of this exercise is to show how much we interfere in normal circumstances and how pervasive this interference is. When it drops away, even for a brief moment, remarkable things begin to show up in people. In essence, the exercise reveals our real putting stroke and allows us to develop a deeper trust in ourselves as putters.

The exercise also breaks up the myth of "If I think the right thoughts, I'll hit the ball better and make more putts." It undermines the thinking/analyzing/conceptualizing mind. It challenges the belief that "thinking (the right thoughts) produces (the right) action." This concept controls most golfers' practice sessions and is a barrier to real development. When we consider that when the mind is distracted from thinking about how to putt, the body can then do the putting on its own, it reverses our assumptions about who's in control and reveals a deep and profound learning system/mechanism. It promotes a sense of "other than mind," pointing us to an appreciation of our body's innate abilities, an amazing part of ourselves that we rarely experience directly.

STEP TWO: LOOKING AT THE HOLE

Now that you've added numbers and can see/experience that it's possible to putt without remembering a tip or technique, what's next? Let's move to the second part of the exercise, which you can do without a partner.

• *Freedom Exploration Exercise #3b* •
Looking at the Hole

Address a ball about 4 feet from a hole. When you are ready to putt, turn your head to look at the hole and focus on an area at the back of the hole. Putt while keeping your eyes and focus there, and do not look back at the ball. The quality of your attention on the hole is what's important here.

Can your mind be interested in a blade of grass at the back of the hole? Perhaps it's a spec of dirt or the rim of the cup that gets your attention. What creates fascination with the back of the hole for you? Are you able to focus on that and be as fully engaged as you were with adding the numbers? The benefits of this exercise are not only to be able to free you up but also to get you more in touch with the target.

STEP THREE: LOOKING AT THE BALL
The ultimate purpose of this three-step progression is to connect to the target without looking at it. All great putters I have spoken with have this type of connection.

• *Freedom Exploration Exercise #3c* •
Connecting to the Target
Address a ball about 4 feet from a hole. Turn your head to look at the hole and focus on an area at the back of the hole. Then look at the ball, keeping the sense of connection with the target, and putt. Notice if the connection to the target is similar to when you were looking at the hole.

Can you maintain the same sense of the target when you look at the ball on the green? Can you stay connected to the target even though your eyes are not on it?

This connection to the target is crucial for putting but is difficult to convey in language. A student once asked, "How can I start developing my connection to the target?" I said, "Imagine you haven't seen your husband in a year and you know he's coming today. And while I'm saying this last sentence, you hear the sound of his footsteps approaching. Even though your eyes are on me, what are you connected to?" "To him, of course!" she replied. Well, that's what I mean by connection. When you're connected you don't have to explain it. The important thing is to be aware when you are and when you're not.

Ben Crenshaw is said to have commented that when he putts well he smells the dirt at the bottom of the cup. Now I don't know if that's literally true or not, but it's certainly an indication of a strong connection with the target. So the intention is to develop a relationship with the target even though you're not looking at it, since the eyes are not the only way to establish such a connection. It's possible to look at things and not be with them, and also to not look at things and still be with them. When you can be with the ball and yet are fully connected to the target, putting is not a big deal.

To recap the exercises . . .

1. Reacting spontaneously to the hole (the target) while adding numbers
2. Creating your own fascination with the target by looking at the hole and noticing if this fascination allows for the same spontaneous reactive freedom
3. Moving the eyes from the hole to the ball, being connected to the target (hole) and noticing if the freedom is the same as in the first exercise

The first exercise (fingers) shows what's possible. The other two can be compared to that exercise. In other words, are you as free, spontaneous and connected in all?

INTERLUDE:
ONE SHOT EXAMINED

I was an English major in college. Part of our curriculum included reading some of the world's great novels and discerning what makes them so. One criterion of a great novel, we learned, is that the reader can see the whole of the novel in its first pages. The theme, tone and structure of the first part of the book portend what is to come. Simply stated, every part of the book leads to the whole and you can get the whole from every part.

This could be said to be true about golf—that we can get the theme and structure of our whole game by thoroughly examining one shot from beginning to end. One shot can open up the whole thing. Let's look at how this is possible.

A shot starts with an intention, a vision. This could be

an overall vision for your game (such as to be a person who swings freely in all situations), or one for that particular shot (I intend to start the putt on the right side of the cup).

I've asked many golfers if they create a clear intention, and most admit that they don't. When I query them about why this is the case, their answers, after quite a bit of conversation, usually come down to the following: They don't like a clear intention because if they intend something and it doesn't happen, they see themselves as having failed. This is another way of saying that they have difficulty coping with failure. It is truly amazing how as human beings we stop ourselves from doing remarkable things because of the fear of failing, of being wrong and of what our minds might make of it.

When an intention is clearly created, the next step becomes logical: Where have we chosen to put our attention *during* the action? In other words, what's our commitment? Of the thousands of areas to which we could pay attention, where have we chosen to do so, so that we might be present to the action and learn from it?

A commitment consistent with one of the above intentions (to be a person who swings freely in all situations) might be to experience one's upper body throughout the swing, and to notice whether or not it is free. A commitment consistent with the other intention (to start the putt on the right side of the cup) might be to be connected with the right side of the cup throughout the stroke.

So first there is an intention. Then there is a place to put our attention during the action. If we don't clearly choose a place to put our attention, the default place that our mind typically provides is "How do I look?" or "Did I perform well?"—trapping us in self-judgments and evaluations of outcomes.

First *in*tention, then *at*tention. Then the action takes place. We putt.

After the action, when the movement has ended, the question becomes, "What happened?" Did we keep our attention where we intended, or not? Did we keep our commitment? Or did something displace it?"

It's amazing to ask these questions because typically our mind attempts to wriggle out of a clear answer by distracting us with stories. But to simply answer whether we kept our attention where we intended and notice when our attention shifted is a powerful practice, requiring diligence and attentiveness. This is called the "debrief" of the shot.

The debrief takes place 2 to 3 seconds after the putt is hit because that's how long it takes for feedback to process through the system. The debrief of the shot can include what we learned, where the breakdown occurred and the thoughts that interfered with our attention. Or it could be an assessment of how strong our commitment was in the first place.

By the way, these three areas—intention, commitment and debrief—also have correspondences in business: leadership, management and coaching.

Leadership is creating a vision—an intention—and the energy to move into action.

Management pays attention to what is happening while the action takes place, focusing on keeping actions in line with the commitment of the group.

Coaching reflects upon—debriefs—what happened so that we may learn from it.

STEP BY STEP

What happens with most golfers is that the intention is vague, the commitment isn't chosen and the debrief ends up being a judgment along the lines of good, bad, right or wrong. Let's take this into real time with a shot, a coach and a student.

The player steps up to the ball.

COACH: What do you intend to do?

PLAYER: I intend to putt freely.

COACH: Where do you plan on putting your attention while you putt? In other words, what's your commitment?

STUDENT: My commitment is to put my attention on my arms and hands and to notice the freedom or tension in them during the stroke.

COACH: Okay. That's clear.

The student putts.

COACH: What happened during the action [putting]?

STUDENT: [*the examination takes a few moments*] I lost awareness of my hands and arms.

COACH: What then became your target? What was your true intention, the one you were connected to? The one that was hidden when you started?

STUDENT: During the putt I was concerned with "Better make it or it'll be embarrassing."

COACH: And with the attention to the thought "Better make it . . ." what happened then?

STUDENT: I can see now that I lost all feel. I judged impact as soon as I hit it. I looked up quickly to see the outcome and whether I was going to be embarrassed.

COACH: Given the change of attention from feeling your arms and hands to "better make it," did the stroke change?

STUDENT: Yes. I can see now that it became jerky and quick, and I noticed that I left the putter face open.

If the practice stroke and the ball stroke are different, it reveals that our intention has changed—our target has changed. In a golf program, we use the word "breakdown" to describe this change. A breakdown doesn't indicate a mishit but rather a loss of commitment in the midst of the action. In other words, I intended my attention to be on a particular thing, but during the stroke my attention moved elsewhere without my realizing it. In Extraordinary Golf, a breakdown is not a failure but simply a "breaking down," an unconscious change of the original commitment.

One of the first things we ask of people in a program is to start noticing where their attention goes, to be aware if they are aware of what's happening. One golf shot can tell a lot about everything. Students may find that they aren't very strong with their commitments, that they lose them in the midst of the action. They may find that they hold commitment like a burden, something that they have to try to do. Such explorations have shown that a real commitment might be the only true freedom—the freedom to act with focus and clarity.

As a golf coach, I've noticed that when the intention changes, the swing changes. And when the swing changes, of course the outcome varies. One of the intentions of coaching, and one aspect of training people to self-coach, is to have students experience the heretofore unnoticed interplay between intention and outcome. The new default commitments that the students take on show that they, like most of us, are quite adept at hiding the truth from themselves. It's easy to tell what they're really committed to by the first thing that comes out of their mouths after a shot is hit. All we have to do is listen. Very few people hit a shot and say, "Ooh! I was connected to the target." "Oops, I just lost my connection to the target." "That was really free." "There was a high degree of trust" or "I really felt the clubhead." Most say, "That was terrible!" "I looked up!" or some other emotional story about the shot. What they say shows what they got—where they put their true attention.

In order to increase awareness and the ability to self-coach, creating a new language can be helpful. Here are some key terms:

Intention: a created design, a vision.

Commitment: a choice of where to place our awareness in the midst of the action.

Breakdown: a loss or unconscious change of commitment in the midst of the action.

Debrief: a time to unfold the learning, to assess what actually happened during the two seconds of the golf stroke. It's an opportunity to revisit the commitment and contrast it to what actually happened.

You know why golf appears to be so difficult for most people? Because we aren't trained in this process. Have you attended Commitment School? Received a master's in intention? A Ph.D. in handling breakdowns and coming back to your true commitment?

My point is that if we fully and honestly examine one shot, from beginning to end, we're well on our way to making a difference in our whole game because golf is simply a series of single shots. And if we upgrade the quality of our awareness in this particular shot, the one that's happening in the present (the only one that matters), we will learn something from the shot, and by so learning our performance tomorrow will be upgraded.

Tomorrow's performance and enjoyment rest on today's learning.

Chapter Seven

FREEDOM EXPLORATION #4: ENJOYING THE MOTION

A few years ago when I was in Japan working with a group of students, an interesting question occurred to me and I asked the group: "How many of you enjoy your putting motion? Not the result but just the movement *itself*?"

I was stunned when no one said that they actually enjoyed their motion—not a single person. I asked the same question about their full swing and no one enjoyed that either. They liked the feeling of hitting it solidly or when they felt the swing was "right," and sometimes they liked the results, but no one actually enjoyed the motion itself.

I then asked a lady in the group to make any motion she enjoyed. She thought for a while and then moved her hand

and her body a bit, like a waving motion back and forth, and said she liked that. I asked her if it felt good, and she responded that it did. So for the next thirty minutes we took that hand motion and developed a putting stroke out of it.

The premise is that if you don't enjoy the stroke itself, the results will be less than you want. Most people suffer and work hard in order to get a result, and assume that this is the only way to succeed. What would it be like if you switched that around and the purpose of putting was simply to enjoy the movement itself? It's possible to hit a ball on the toe or the heel, high or low on the blade and still enjoy the motion, or hit a 10-footer 3 feet past the hole and sincerely have the movement feel great to you. We're so conditioned to label a putt as "wrong" if we don't hit it on the right part of the club or if we don't get the result we wanted, that we don't actually experience the movement, let alone enjoy it. We wait for the moment when it actually touches the club to make a judgment about whether or not it was good, or whether we enjoyed it. It's too late then— much too late.

When you ask remarkable players, men or women, whether they like how their swing feels, a high percentage say they do. So what would happen if we made the enjoyment of the motion the criterion for evaluation of the swing? The kind of awareness that allows you to sense whether or not you enjoy the motion is a high learning state. I'll call it a blend of awareness and enjoyment.

As you read this you may say, "If it's just about the motion and not the result, how will I know if I like it?" You'll know because it will resonate in your body like a tuning fork. Find a movement that feels good in your body all the way to the end. Move back and forth until you simply like what you do, to the point where you want to keep on doing it. I think you will find it quite fascinating.

Is it possible for you to be in that state all the way through the motion? If you don't enjoy your golf swing, no one else will. It's uncomfortable to watch many people putt because their motion seems anything but enjoyable—often stressful and awkward. But people who seem to like their swing usually produce something that is efficient, effortless, easy, graceful and free.

FREE AND EASY

Finding something you enjoy is one of the best ways to develop freedom. And for something to be free, it needs to be enjoyed for itself alone, rather than for the result that you get from it.

Now I'm not inviting you to abdicate performance—quite the contrary. I assure you that I have as much interest in performing as you do. But after forty thousand golf lessons and forty-eight years of playing, I've seen that worrying about performance does not lead to improved performance. Focusing on learning and enjoyment yields far richer results. Most of us are so addicted to performance that in its pursuit we'll endure all kinds of suffering, and even abandon learning. As a matter of fact, learning is often seen as something to endure in order to perform. However, suffering is not required.

I suggest that you find a motion you enjoy first in a small version (short putts), and then take it to a larger version (longer putts). Find a small motion that just feels good to your body. Begin to notice if you feel stress as the putts get longer. Is there any tightening? Jerkiness? What would it be like to have a putting stroke that feels great from beginning to end, no matter what happens? What if you never gave up freedom or joy of motion for the result? That would take a lot of courage, but it's the only way I have found that things repeat in a consistent manner. Real freedom is consistent.

All the mechanics of the stroke—how the arms hinge at the shoulders, whether the putter face goes back open, closed or square, the acceleration of the putter—can be put on hold for now. Simply stay with the question of whether or not you enjoy it. The freedom that comes from enjoying the motion is the foundation of a great putting stroke, and this is also true for every swing in golf. Great players love the movement itself, how it feels. I swing in my garage just to make the movement of a full swing or putting stroke because I like it, much like dancers love dancing for its own sake, not just for the result. Can you just enjoy the movement and differentiate it from the joy of the result?

• *Freedom Exploration Exercise #4a* •
Enjoying the Motion

Make your normal putting motion and, without using a ball, notice if the motion feels enjoyable to you from beginning to end. Let go of the mechanics for now and simply notice how your body feels while making this putting stroke. If it isn't completely enjoyable, experiment until you find a motion that is. The goal is to find a putting motion that is so enjoyable you would do it for its own sake.

The next step is to take this swing out to the practice putting green or to the golf course and see if you can still accurately discern whether you enjoy the stroke itself. You'll quickly realize how much attention is required to experience the physical motion until the end of the swing. The challenge of this exercise is to stay present to your body until the end, and not evaluate how you did in the shot or whether you exhibited sound mechanics. Stay conscious of your intention and motion.

Here's a good way to test your level of intention. Imagine the following scenario: You start a round with the goal of focusing only on the enjoyment of the putting motion, and find yourself with a downhill 10-foot putt for par on the first green. Do you have the courage to be present and set aside your considerations about performance at this point? Can you stay with your body to the end of the putting motion, discerning your enjoyment of the stroke? What would this require?

Here's a suggestion: Keep a separate "enjoyment score" on your scorecard, with a 10 for "I enjoyed it fully and it was a free motion," down to a 1 for "I guided it, steered it, manipulated it/did not enjoy it." It will help keep you in the game of awareness and enjoyment rather than in the game of performance. We all know the performance game, since it's the one in which we usually find ourselves, whether we want it or not. It's the one that connects our self-worth, and corresponding self-esteem, with our golf score. I suggest you do not use this enjoyment of motion exercise as merely another tip or swing thought to increase performance. Let enjoyment of the motion be the sole criterion, and the results will take care of themselves. Can you have enough awareness of the experience to rate it?

· *Freedom Exploration Exercise #4b* ·
Enjoying the Motion with the Target

Take this motion out to the practice putting green or to the golf course and see if you have enough awareness to accurately determine whether you enjoy the stroke itself. You'll quickly realize how much attention is required to experience the physical motion until the end of the swing. The challenge of this exercise is to stay present to your body until the end, not to evaluate how you did in the shot or whether you exhibited sound mechanics. Stay conscious of your intention and motion.

When you're on the course, consider keeping a separate putting "enjoyment score" on your scorecard, with a range from 10 (high enjoyment of the stroke) to 1 (low enjoyment).

To sum up this exercise: It is about becoming present to your body from beginning to end of the stroke. The quality of your attention is the key ingredient here. Were you aware enough to discern whether you enjoyed the motion?

It is possible to love the game of golf not just for the result, or for the time between shots, but for the simple joy a free motion can bring.

Chapter Eight

FREEDOM EXPLORATION #5:
EXPOSING INTERFERENCE

When you find a putting stroke that you really love, one that feels smooth, free and easy, what's next? It's obvious! You watch yourself mess it up! Or to put it a bit less flippantly, you discover how you interfere with your freedom.

• *Freedom Exploration Exercise #5* •
Exposing Interference

Find a partner, then go to a putting green with a bucket of balls and set the bucket on the green a few feet in from the edge. It doesn't matter where the nearest hole is, since you won't be putting to a hole at first. Have your friend kneel down by the bucket while you take a putting stance a few feet away. Your partner should be able to take a ball out of the bucket and place it where you can putt it.

You, the putter, simply swing back and forth with a putting stroke at the same height above the ground as if you were striking a ball. Continue back and forth without stopping until you find that free, enjoyable stroke. Tell your partner when you've found it and keep swinging.

Your partner then takes a ball and either places it so you strike it (while you continue your ongoing motion like a pendulum) or fakes placing it on the ground and takes it back at the last moment. Your job, as the putter, is to continue without stopping. Your partner's job is to place balls periodically at a frequency that's unpredictable to you.

We often do this exercise in our golf program with a coach placing the golf balls. About 95 percent of the time the people putting alter their stroke when a ball is placed in front of them. There is usually a noticeable flinch. The people watching will often laugh at the sudden shift. If I remove the ball just before the person gets to impact, the

EXPOSING INTERFERENCE—
WITHDRAWING THE BALL

EXPOSING INTERFERENCE—
PLACING THE BALL

stroke will also become jerky, or it may move on a different line. Oftentimes it slows down when the ball is there.

I let students know that I am not going to touch them, and I won't stop their motion or disrupt it in any way. All I'll do is feed balls in an unpredictable pattern. I ask them if they can just keep going back and forth with their motion no matter what I do, and students typically say they can. But they don't. As soon as I put a ball down they change. Most often they jab at the ball. This "jab" stroke, the one that's different from their natural stroke, is the one they've been using on the golf course, unbeknownst to them. They take the putting stroke they love and change it in the midst of the action. It's fascinating. I continue with the exercise, all the time coaching them not to do anything but observe the interference.

So have your putting partner keep placing balls so you get the opportunity to see how your stroke changes. Can you catch it? How much does it change? Where in your body does it change? Do you tighten your hands? Your shoulders? Your fingers? Do you jab at the ball or alter the line? This altered putting stroke is probably the one you have been putting with every time you play. It's just now exposed.

When you can really experience the interference, in the moment it happens, you've started winning—and developing. Usually our self-interference is hidden from us, and so we don't experience it. We experience the *result* of the interference—tight muscles and a jerky stroke—but never the genesis of it. Where does it actually begin? In what part of our body? The wonderful, free putting strokes that are possible for all people are rarely used on the golf course, and golfers rarely notice that they are not used. Even more rare is for people to experience how they interfere with them. The path to freedom in putting is not in avoiding the interference or in pretending that it is an issue of technique, but rather in exposing the interference, bringing it out in the open.

Students in our workshops typically say, "Now that I've experienced the interference, what do I do next?" There is such a strong tendency to want to fix something. But the goal here is to simply keep watching it. Get to know it. See if you can let go of the judgment that interference is bad and freedom is good. If you experience both the freedom and the interference without judgment, you won't have to choose which is better. Your body will choose. It happens every time. Trust me.

No . . . trust yourself.

Chapter Nine.

FREEDOM EXPLORATION #6: REACTION PUTTING

One of the big complaints people have about golf is that because there's so much time between shots, there's too much time to think. Whereas tennis, baseball, football and basketball are reaction sports, golf takes place somewhat statically, without ongoing action/reaction. The perception seems to be that if there's more time to think there's more chance for interference, and so it's more difficult to perform. I find it very interesting that during the last decade in the static part of basketball—free throws—performance at almost all levels has declined despite the increased knowledge and technology. More information but less performance. I see the same thing in golf.

I had a powerful insight on this issue of dynamic versus

static motion a number of years ago when a close friend came to me about a problem in his swing. He described how his left arm bent on his downswing and through impact, causing him to lose a lot of power and accuracy. He had tried everything he could think of—including strapping on a piece of cardboard tubing—to try to keep his arm straight, but to no avail. I filmed him hitting balls on the range, and sure enough, his arm was bent. He told me that this had been going on for thirty years.

It happened that I had recently been exploring a new exercise in which I would hit balls that someone rolled to me from the side about 10 feet away. I found that after a short while I could hit the balls just as solidly when they were rolling as when they were sitting still—the same in the dynamic mode as in the static mode. As a matter of fact, I found I could even hit balls more solidly when they were rolling, and this bewildered me. How was this possible? It didn't seem logical, yet I could sense an increase of freedom when I was hitting a rolling ball. However, I hadn't filmed it yet.

I invited my friend (with the bent left arm at impact) to hit some rolling golf balls. I rolled twenty balls at him and while at first he hit some and missed some, after a short time he started to hit them all fairly solidly. I had the camera on a tripod and filmed him. Afterward we watched the film in slow motion and stop-action to see what his body was doing. What we saw was remarkable: For nineteen of the twenty balls he hit, his arm was as straight as an iron beam! The one ball he hit with a bent arm was the ball that had bounced across the grass and stopped for about one second before he hit it. This was stunning. His arm had bent with a still ball but responded differently with balls in motion. How could it be that a person could spend thirty years trying to straighten his arm without success, yet do so easily while hitting rolling balls without trying?

This was intriguing, to say the least. I've since filmed many people hitting rolling golf balls—in putting, chipping and the full swing—to see what happens. The pattern has been consistent with what I saw in my friend that day. While initially people may not hit the ball more solidly, with every person, including myself, the technique improved immediately *every time*. This has given me a whole new perspective on how we learn, how our bodies move and what's possible if we get out of our heads and simply respond to what's in front of us. It has been a revelation.

So if we were to learn golf dynamically, could we let go of our interference and discover more of our natural swing? Perhaps. The only way to find out is to try it. You will need a partner, and the two of you should switch halfway through so each can experience both roles. The setup is a little different in putting than it is in the full swing.

• *Freedom Exploration Exercise #6a* •
Reaction Putting

Find a partner and stand on the green about 6 feet apart, facing each other. Your partner has a putter and you have a golf ball. Roll a ball at moderate speed to your partner and have him putt it back to you. The goal is not to hit any particular spot, just to hit the ball back in your general direction. Ask your partner to notice how his body feels, what tension exists,

REACTION PUTTING: ROLLING
THE BALL TO THE STUDENT

REACTION PUTTING: STUDENT
PUTTING THE BALL BACK

what part of his body is being used. Ask him to feel the pacing of the stroke. Roll the ball to him about twenty times, then switch so that you, too, can experience the exercise.

Talking and writing about this exercise won't be as interesting as seeing it. We find that people's hands change, as does their putting stroke. Softness emerges. This exercise is designed to strip down the motion and have the person putting experience their stroke when they are not affecting it—not manipulating the motion or trying to remember a formula. They simply respond to the ball coming at them, and notice what's going on. Once again, there will be something that's fascinating and different from the normal stroke.

How does it feel to be reactive and spontaneous and to let go? What is this sense of freedom like? When the mind is occupied with having to adjust to a moving ball, it's amazing what the body can do. My honest opinion after all these years is that golf would be easier to learn if the ball were rolling.

We now add a target to the mix and, as in previous exercises, observe if the presence of the target changes the motion.

• *Freedom Exploration Exercise #6b* •
Reaction Putting to a Hole

This is the same scenario as the previous exercise, with both people about 6 feet apart, except that the person rolling the ball is next to a hole. Have your partner roll a ball to you and putt it back to him as before. Notice the experience. Then instead of hitting the next ball right back to him, stop the ball with your putter, take a very short pause and then putt it back toward the hole. Notice if there is a difference between this experience and the previous one. Continue this pattern of first hitting a rolling ball then stopping the ball, pausing and putting it toward the hole, noticing the differences. Gradually let the balls you stop rest for a longer time before you putt them. Then switch roles.

Were the actions of putting a rolling ball to your partner and a resting ball to the hole similar? Did you just react or was there thinking and calculation when hitting the stationary ball? If you begin to get a feeling of just responding to a stationary ball, with little thinking, let the ball stop for a longer time before putting it to a target. Lengthen the time that the ball sits before you putt it to a target until the ball sits for four or five seconds before you hit it.

There is no telling what you and your partner will learn from this exercise. People have varying experiences, but the most important thing is to examine the experience. What does it tell you? When a ball lies in front of you, are you different than when it rolls at you? Can you have a stroke that is reactive, spontaneous and free when the ball isn't moving? Can you get ready, line up the putt and step up and hit it as if it were moving, as if there's nothing to remember, just react to a target? Can you trust that your body will know how far to hit it in the same way it knows how to throw a Frisbee and toss a ball? Compare who you are and what you feel in both circumstances, dynamic and static.

This exercise is designed to have you experience the genius of your body and how trustworthy it is. Perhaps with this new awareness you might develop the intention and courage to simply let go to a target when on the golf course.

FREEDOM EXPLORATIONS: SUMMARY

When we ask our Extraordinary Golf participants what real freedom might look like, they say, "Freedom to let it go. Freedom to trust myself. Freedom to be myself and to know that I am enough. Freedom to recognize clearly the barriers I put up—the interference—and to get them out in the open so I can deal with them."

If any of these exercises have opened up a doorway to that kind of freedom for you, keep going. A deeper exploration can produce miracles. Being human means that we have undergone millions of years of evolution and have resources and assets that are almost beyond what we can imagine. Without a doubt, our body is worthy of trust.

INTERLUDE:
THE STORY OF GOLF

2004 PGA SUMMIT

I attended the 2004 Coaching & Teaching Summit of the PGA, and it was a fascinating event. More than a thousand golf teaching professionals assembled for three days of learning.

It occurred to me upon arrival that I was coming to a "cultural event" and that I could learn something about the people of my culture—the culture of golfers. Since I arrived early, and I was to give an hour-long talk to the group at the end of the second and third days, I had almost two full days to interact with fellow golf pros before I spoke. I could observe and ask them questions, and their responses would reveal the very nature and foundation of our golf culture.

I asked questions of dozens of golf professionals, the first of which was, "What is the most important aspect of coaching and teaching? In other words, what should I talk about?" The answers to this question would reveal the perceived priorities and direction of our profession.

The second question was, "What would you have to learn and develop to be paid five hundred dollars an hour five years from now, and have your students comment that you're well worth that kind of fee?" The answers would provide a sense of vision of their future and their development.

The curriculum for the three days spanned developing more power, short game and full swing technique, how to spot faults and provide fixes, how to teach women, the use of new technology and teaching the fundamentals. As I listened to the speakers and to the answers the professionals gave me, the underlying belief at the foundation of our golf culture began to emerge.

The rules of most games are usually well defined. In bowling, the game is to score as high as possible so that in a competition, the highest score wins. In golf, the game is to score as low as possible, and the lowest scoring player wins. Yet the purpose of golf has not been defined. Each golfer must choose that for him/herself.

Clearly, the PGA Coaching & Teaching Summit—this cultural event—implied something about the purpose of the game. The purpose of the game was revealed in the presenters' words and in the audience's conversations during the sessions and the breaks. The purpose of the game, the foundation for instruction and the core belief of this culture became obvious. And it is this:

If I get a better swing, and better scores, I will be happier.

That message was broadcast every hour onstage. It was talked about in the audience and was the underlying theme of dinner conversations. "If our students get better, they'll be happier."

When it came my turn to talk, I decided to test the validity of this assumption directly with the audience. I said, "There are about one thousand pros sitting here now, probably the largest gathering of low-scoring players in the world this year. You are the epitome of what you think our students are asking for. *You* have gotten better. You have reached the heights of performance in a way only a few of our students will. I have to ask you . . . Are you happy? Are you satisfied and full of joy about your game? Do you have peace of mind? Do you experience a deep connection with your playing partners and an appreciation of nature? Did it all turn out for you from 'getting better'?"

Of course, they started to laugh. They're very bright men and women who know that "getting better" is a big myth. That "getting better" doesn't create the kind of happiness that people hope for. The key belief—the foundation—of golf instruction in this country (if I get better, I will be happier) has never proven to be real. It's just a belief.

I'm also very careful not to imply the opposite—i.e., that better scores have no effect. I'm well aware of the temporary effect a low score has. It's like buying anything new—clothes, cars, even houses—that makes you feel good at first, but only for a while, often a short while.

What I am saying is that enjoyment and performance can be *unlinked.* In other words, enjoyment is not dictated by performance (whether performance is defined as hitting well or scoring low). Enjoyment is not a function of performance. Once we make that separation, new dimensions of learning and enjoyment (and, ironically, performance) are possible.

Getting back to my second question ("What would make you worth five hundred dollars an hour . . .), most pros answered they had no idea. Those who did answer said that they'd have to be better and faster at seeing faults and providing fixes.

If we deconstruct the myth that fixing faults and getting better will get people what they really want (freedom, peace of mind, joy . . . even self-coaching), then we are free to start exploring what they're really seeking.

LIKE GOLF, LIKE LIFE

Our golf culture is simply one aspect of the far-reaching culture that surrounds us, and the two share core beliefs. The most fundamental belief in the dominant business culture, and that which directly parallels the one in golf, is as follows: better productivity = more happiness. This key assumption seems unquestioned with the many companies we've worked with and those we read about. But is it true? My personal experience tells me that it isn't, as does my assessment of the world around me. In addition, no statistical data that I have seen has proven this belief to be true. As a matter of fact, a strong case may be made for the opposite.

Productivity in this country has risen dramatically in the last twenty years, and along with it has come greater stress and less overall satisfaction for most people. Productivity has led to the desire for more productivity, not happiness.

The same is seen in golf: No level of "getting better" is satisfactory. The fact that I've gotten better doesn't change the conditioned expectation that I've got to get better and better. It could be argued that success in the performance realm is failure because it leads to more wanting and to the belief that "more" is the key to happiness and overall satisfaction.

We've had many discussions with people about this, and even those who clearly acknowledge the falseness—the myth—of that equation (productivity = happiness) have great difficulty conceiving of another way to operate, to do business or to make a living. Among golf professionals I hear the corollary, "I know that getting better isn't the source of happiness, but it's the only story we have."

HAVE WE REALLY IMPROVED?

A few years ago, I led a workshop for the Southern Ohio PGA. Before I started I asked the attending pros three questions:

1. In all the time you've been in the golf business, have you seen people improve, *really*? Are people better now than they were back then?
2. In all this time, have you seen people get more joy out of the game? If golfers wore a "Joy Meter" on their shirt collar, would it show them to be scoring higher on enjoyment?

3. Are golfers better able to coach themselves? Do they have a greater capacity to learn now than when you started teaching?

There were ten tables with six pros sitting at each table. They talked among themselves for a while and then shared their conclusions. Ten out of ten tables answered no to my first question: People aren't better than they were ten, twenty or thirty years ago. Ten out of ten tables answered that people are not enjoying the game any more. And, nine out of ten tables answered that people are no more able to learn now than they were back then. One table answered yes to this question due to increased access to technology and drills. Their peers shouted them down.

So I asked, "If the golfing experience encompasses learning, enjoyment and performance, you're saying that you've not seen significant impact in those three areas in your time in this business. Is that true?" They answered yes. So I said, "If what you're saying is true and we spend the day exploring in the same paradigm and expect different results, then we're all crazy." (I didn't ask those three questions to the pros at the PGA Coaching & Teaching Summit, and I wonder what their responses might have been. My experience tells me their answers would have been very similar.)

The most significant, observable result from all the attention and worry we place on "getting better" (at the expense of enjoyment and learning) is that golfers really don't improve. Learning is seen as something to get past in order to get better, and the average handicap has stayed the same for fifty years.

It's ironic that when golfers focus on getting better, they don't. Yet when they attend to—keep their eye on and cultivate—joy and learning, they improve rapidly. So if being driven to get better doesn't really produce happiness, and if scoring lower doesn't really add richness to life (which at some level must be the purpose of golf), then what allows for happiness, peace of mind, joy and satisfaction?

For fifteen years, the coaches and students of Extraordinary Golf have explored that question. Here's some of what we've learned along the way.

Part Two

PEACE OF MIND EXPLORATIONS

At one point in an Extraordinary Golf program, the coaches play a round of golf with the students and ask that the students play a hole in complete silence, without uttering a single word to themselves, other students or the coach. Once the last ball is putted in, the coach invites the students to reflect and comment on this experience. What was it like? Was it quiet? More often than not, students report that while the group played in silence, their mind was far from quiet—there was a great deal of internal chatter. The normal conversation of a golf round tends to obscure this, but once people stop talking and start listening to their minds it becomes clear that the chatter occurs almost all the time. Further listening will amplify this internal dialogue to the point of being able to hear complete sentences, unfolding paragraphs and full dramas. Experience has shown that this is true not just for those students, but also for all of us.

Each human being has a quiet conversation inside his or her head, one that takes place at some level almost constantly. I'm not talking about the kind of thinking that is intentional, generative and creative, the kind that arises in response to unique situations in our life and assists us in acting. I'm talking about the automatic, repetitive chatter, the kind that seems pretty much the same day after day and interferes with our actions. We'll call this the Voice in our head. While the existence of this Voice is obvious to some who've taken the time to observe it, to others it may not be. Sometimes, participants in our program start out saying, "I don't have a Voice saying anything." By the end of the program they're amazed at how they could have been unaware of it. This Voice seems to be almost automatic, continually commenting on anything and everything. You can experience it now. It's the same Voice that breaks your attention and causes you to drift away from the book as you read. I think that a great deal of what we all do for entertainment—radio, TV, etc.— is motivated by the desire to escape from its constant chatter. Yet there are times when the Voice seems to quiet down and our minds become more clear and peaceful. Students describe these as their best days. The next exercises are about a way of being with the Voice that allows for great putting, great golf and the possibility of greater peace of mind.

Chapter Ten

PEACE OF MIND
EXPLORATION #1:
THE VOICE

On the putting green, we have students place a ball one inch from a cup and simply putt it. We ask them, "Was there any doubt, any fear?" In all the years of doing this, rarely has anyone said that they had any doubt when the ball almost hangs on the lip of the cup. They just tap it in.

This leads to the question, "How would we know if we have doubt? What form does doubt take?" Students have said that they feel nervous or scared, and when I ask them to describe those feelings they reply that their body is shaky and their chest is constricted. I point out that those physical sensations are very similar to what they feel when cold or excited. It becomes clear that doubt is something more than just a physical sensation, so what else is there? After some reflection, students usually say, "There would also be a little voice in my head saying something to me."

So if doubt is a "Voice" and that Voice isn't talking to us at one inch from the hole, we'll call that a state of "no doubt." This experience becomes our benchmark. We then ask the students to start moving the ball away from the hole in 6-inch increments, putting each time. Their job is to notice the very first moment when something other than "no doubt" creeps in. When does some thought or voice show up that wasn't there at one inch? When does the internal experience start to differ?

It does not take long for the Voice to show up with its intrusions and comments. I think we are all too familiar with the things that it typically says: "Don't miss—it will be embarrassing." "Make sure it's not short." Or you might hear a piece of internal "coaching" such as, "Relax. Be smooth. Back of the left hand to the hole." Or even some "positive thinking" phrases such as, "You can make this." The point is that whether negative or positive, it is different from the benchmark. There was nothing one inch from the hole, but there is something at some distance away. From my experience this happens to everyone, and it's amazing all the things that come up. The goal of this exercise is to notice when the Voice starts its commentary and to note what it says.

• *Peace of Mind Exploration* •
Exercise #1: The Voice

Place a ball on the putting green one inch from a cup, address it in your normal way and putt it in. Notice if there is any doubt—any voice in your head. Repeat this several times, and use this experience as a baseline. Then move the ball away from the hole in 6-inch increments, putting it each time. Notice when the experience first begins to differ from the baseline, and what form this difference takes.

It's not the occurrence of the Voice that's the major problem, but the fact that we usually take what it says seriously and feel the need to follow it or counter it. The fact that we engage with it diverts our attention and creates the interference that so hampers our enjoyment and performance. It's crucial to bring this inner dialogue to light.

During this exercise in a golf program a student typically hears mental commentary—the Voice—for the first time when the ball is around 18 inches from the hole. He or she reports this to the coach, who describes the situation for the class. For example, "So you have an eighteen-inch putt and the commentary in your head says, 'Don't miss it to the right.' What do you do next?" Having asked this type of question to many people over the years, we've heard a fascinating array of coping strategies in response. People typically say something like, "If I hear the Voice tell me I'll miss it to the right, then I'll check my alignment and make sure I follow through straight to the hole." Or, "I back off and come back again." Or, "If the Voice tells me I can't make it, I tell it I *can* make it."

Most people react to what the Voice tells them to do. They think the Voice is a valid reminder and that they need to abide by what it says. Yet when we ask whether this has proven to be a good thing to do over the course of the years, whether this approach has provided greater peace of mind and freedom, almost everyone says no, even when the Voice's comments were "positive." This brings up an important distinction.

POSITIVE THINKING

It's easy for people to accept the fact that negative thinking can be a source of interference. I've found that the real challenge is to have people see for themselves that positive thinking can be just as much of a problem. My experience of positive thinking is that it's just more thinking, a *mental* process while we're in a *physical* activity. It's also an indicator of doubt. Look at it this way: Anything that you really trust in your life, you don't think negatively—or positively—about, you simply do it. For instance, I don't need to think positively when I walk or drive a car. I don't have to tell myself, "I'm a really great walker and I'm not going to stumble. I can do this." Of course not. When I walk I'm in complete trust of my ability. No Voice of doubt enters my mind, so no coping dialogue is triggered. Positive thinking is an overlay of doubt; it's a strategy to overcome negative thinking, and while it may have better effects than negative thinking, I've never seen it fully promote peace of mind and freedom. It's simply more thinking.

So let's get back to the circumstance of the exercise. A foot and a half away from the cup, a Voice comes in and says, "Don't miss it or it will be embarrassing." If you had a choice of having that thought or *not* having that thought, which would you choose? Most people would rather not have it. So I invite you to stop this Voice. Go ahead, give it a try.

To save you from what could be a lifetime of futility, I'll tell you that my experience has shown that you can't stop the Voice in your head. Many people who have spent a great deal of their lifetime trying to stop it, including years of meditation and other such practices, share this experience. For some reason, the thoughts come and they keep on coming. They seem to rise in our consciousness like bubbles from the bottom of a champagne glass. They don't seem to start anywhere, they just happen. And they can't be stopped. Having automatic thoughts pop up from seemingly nowhere is apparently part of being human.

So if you didn't intend to start the Voice and can't stop it, what *can* you do with it? Let me give a possible answer to this question by means of a story.

LIKE CHILD, LIKE ADULT
By the time I was seven years old, I had been practicing and playing golf quite a bit and was very skilled for my age. I distinctly remember a day at the practice range when two people stood behind me and one said to the other: "Hey, look at that little guy over there. He really hits it far!" At that moment I formed a conclusion that directed my early

golf life: that if I hit the ball far and well, people will admire and like me. So I practiced and practiced, with my Voice continually telling me that story. But you can see the trap, can't you? If I didn't hit it well, then what? So my practice sessions were permeated with a fear of not hitting it well. As a result, a lot of my tournament play in my teens and twenties was about playing well to be respected. The way I hit the ball, I perceived, had a lot to do with what people would think about me. That internal conversation created a lot of interference and doubt during play.

It took me a long time to realize that my sense of self and my performance were not one and the same. As I began to separate the two, I also started to separate the person I refer to as "I" from the Voice in my head. I realized that the Voice was something other than me. I began to see that this Voice would chat on and on about not being good enough and needing to be better, etc., but that I didn't have to buy into it. So instead of being a victim, I started to differentiate myself from the Voice, and found that doing so gave me more freedom and the ability to live more consciously.

A few years ago our Extraordinary Golf team led a workshop for the Canadian PGA, and in attendance was the famous golf pro Moe Norman. If you don't know about Moe, you should know that he was considered the best ball striker in the history of golf, right up there with Ben Hogan. The workshop ended on the driving range with our host inviting Moe to hit some balls for the group, something Moe was asked to do quite often, given his exceptional skill. So we all gathered around him while he demonstrated his unique ability, hitting shot after amazing shot. Then our host turned to me and said, "Fred, would you hit balls for the group?"

You can imagine my feeling. It was like being asked to sing after Pavarotti. But of course I accepted and walked to the tee. There I was, forty-some years later, hitting balls with people watching just as it was when I was seven years old. And there it still was, the Voice in my head, saying the same thing: "If you hit it well you'll be liked. If you hit it poorly you'll lose their respect—and you'll invalidate the whole day's workshop."

But instead of it being the monster that used to devour me (and would greatly interfere with my performance), I could now recognize the Voice as the automatic, repetitive mechanism that it is, and I didn't have to take it seriously. I took a moment to make a conscious choice about what I wanted to be committed to while hitting. In that moment I was able to separate the real me from this automatic Voice that said I must hit it well or else. I made a conscious choice to hit with freedom, a commitment that was more important to me than any results. So I started firing away and loved it. After hitting for a while, I turned to Moe and asked him if I could hit his driver. He nodded and I got to hit Moe Norman's driver—I loved it! Had I listened to the Voice and followed what it said, I'm sure that the day would have been far different.

The good news is that I don't have to stop the Voice. It doesn't cease, but when I'm able to simply hear it, accept it and do nothing with it, the Voice seems to quiet down a lot. I can't have freedom *from* the Voice, but I can have freedom *with* the Voice. And the degree to which I have that freedom is the degree to which my life works. Everywhere.

ENDLESS LOOP

Studies have shown, and I think it's self-evident, that people have a great deal of the same thoughts from day to day. A study by Stanford University a few years ago went as far as to say that we have around 60,000 thoughts per day, 59,500 of which are the same as the day before. This is not necessarily good or bad; it's simply the way it is.

Once we become aware of the automatic thoughts that loop through our minds day after day, we open up the possibility of distinguishing our capacity for real, generative, creative thinking and being able to use our mind to forward our life's intention.

When you begin to notice the nature of the Voice, you see that it is never in the now, the present. It is always making comparisons with a past event or projecting a future one, and most of what it says is critical, judgmental and fearful. According to my Voice I'm never good enough, smart enough, good-looking enough or nice enough, and the next golf shot is not a sure thing. None of it is true, but this has always been the theme of my Voice and I have no indication that it will change. But now my relationship to the Voice is such that peace of mind is possible.

In our culture, when we're faced with something we perceive to be a problem, our tendency is to want to take action and fix it. But with regard to the Voice, the opposite is most effective. I've found that the best course is to do something most of us have never done, which is to do nothing. *NOTHING.* Just let the Voice be. Hear it, recognize it as an automatic mechanism and let it go by.

True peace of mind is not about avoiding the Voice or engaging in the futility of trying to get rid of it; it's about accepting the Voice and not reacting to it. Instead of trying to change it, fix it, outthink it or get away from it, can you just let it be? Can the automatic thoughts in your head be like the wind that just blew by?

RICH REWARDS

So how does this relate to golf and putting? Let's go back to the circumstance of the previous exercise. When the Voice intrudes, can you recognize the intrusion, let it be and come back to what *you* intend at that moment? I think that's where the real power lies. It could mean that you come back to your intention of letting go, of sensing your body, of paying attention to the clubhead—whatever you choose. This won't happen smoothly at first, since the Voice's hold on us can be very strong, but don't worry. Each time you get caught up in the mental story, simply recognize it, cut yourself some slack and come back to your intention. The more you do this, the easier it will become. This new freedom can expand to other areas in your life as well.

This awareness is at the heart of great putting. The Voice itself isn't the source of interference, what we do with it is. Reacting to it, believing it and following it down whatever path it offers are sources of interference. You can start this training right now, as you read this page. You can start noticing when thoughts pull you away from the page and let them go, bringing yourself back to what you intend (reading). The game is to catch ourselves going down that road and be a comeback player.

True peace of mind comes simply from letting go of that which disrupts it. The only thing that disrupts it is this quiet conversation. If you really seek peace of mind, then you will have to deal with the Voice. Your capacity to recognize it, let it be and come back to the task at hand—the one that you have created—is one of the most powerful things any human being can do in golf, or anywhere else.

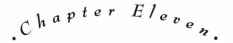

Chapter Eleven

PEACE OF MIND
EXPLORATION #2:
CONCENTRATION

One day many years ago, when I was in my late twenties, I played a round of golf with the same coach that I spoke about at the beginning of the book. One of the things I would often do back then was comment on my shots right after I hit them, especially if I thought I hadn't hit them well. For example, I would hit a tee shot I didn't particularly like and then immediately say something like, "I was too quick, came out of it, left the clubface open." Most people I played with ignored my post-swing comments, but he was the first person to actually listen to me. He said, "I notice that after each shot you say why it happened. But I also notice that it doesn't seem to make a big difference in the subsequent shots." He then turned to me and said very politely, "My suggestion to you is to just shut up." Now this was from a fellow who never said anything like that. I was shocked.

He certainly got my attention, and over time I began to understand why he said what he did. He was trying to wake me up to the possibility that I really didn't know the cause of my mishits—that I was wrongly attributing an effect to a cause when there was no relationship between the two. For some reason I felt I needed to come up with an "explanation" for my shots, so I made up what I thought was a likely story. But this story only helped keep me in the dark about what was really going on.

Here's an example. Let's say a friend says to you, "You know, I'm putting so great and all I'm doing is remembering to keep my body still. That's what's making me putt so well."

Is it really true that thinking about keeping his body still is the source of his great putting? Here's another possibility: "Just keeping my body still" is a key swing thought, one of those supposedly "magic" phrases that are expected to improve your swing. Everyone has swing thoughts and sometimes they even seem to work. But do they *really* work, and how long do they last?

I remember going to a seminar once and hearing a very famous sports psychologist talk about key swing thoughts. After the lecture I asked him, "Is there anything beyond key swing thoughts? We know that these thoughts are things that work temporarily at best, and I've never met anyone who had one that lasted for even one year. So why are we putting all our attention on something that has such a short life span? Is there something that we know that can last longer—say for a lifetime?" He looked at me and said, "If you can answer that, we'll both make a million bucks!"

Why the obsession with key swing thoughts? I feel that a big part of the reason is our cultural view about learning, which is commonly seen as the process of taking in large amounts of information, with the more information, the greater the learning. This information is primarily verbal, particularly in golf, so the essential point of view of learning golf in America can be summarized in one simple statement: "If I think the right thoughts, then I will hit the right shots." The further assumption is that if thinking produces the right results, then thinking immediately prior to swinging will have the best effect.

Of all the things I have observed in more than thirty years of golf coaching, that's the biggest misconception.

EXPIRATION DATES

Before I get into what does make a difference, let's look at the typical life cycle of key swing thoughts.

If we happen to find a key swing thought, or "swing key," that seems to work, we initially experience great joy. Life is good, as everything seems to work out and we might have one of those memorable rounds. And of course we think we've found the answer, and that all we have to do is make sure we keep our stroke smooth and follow through to the hole.

The second time we go out to play or practice, the swing thought may still provide nice results, but it is usually less effective. A few of the old habits will likely start showing up—the ones we used the swing key to remedy in the first place. Even though we feel the magic starting to wear off, we still hope that if we just keep thinking and working on the swing key, our performance will return. But then on the third or fourth day it generally all falls apart. We still use the swing key as before, hoping for a return of the good times, but it doesn't seem to produce any positive results. We drift into frustration, anger and despair. Interestingly enough, what doesn't show up is cynicism about swing keys themselves. We just seem to go looking for another key thought, like a computer searching for a program.

In the famous words of singer Peggy Lee, "Is that all there is?" Are we destined to look for one swing key after another for the rest of our golfing life? Some of these thoughts last only minutes, and if we're lucky one will last a whole week, then back to the drawing board. Is there anything else? Let's take a look at what happened to the fellow with the "Keep my body still" swing key, but this time with a different basic assumption.

SWING THOUGHTS DON'T WORK— PEOPLE DO

I contend that when our friend first got the swing key, for a brief period of time he was completely focused on his body, actually experiencing the body itself. Golf became physical. There was nothing else at the beginning but the clear focus on his body, and a natural ability emerged from simply being present. It was this physical focus that made the difference during this first phase, not the actual swing key. So you might say that for a brief period of time, he interrupted the usual constant stream of thoughts, evaluations and judgments— the interference—and felt the sense of calmness and clarity that comes with being present to something physical, some- thing real. As we've said many times in this book, there is a world of difference between simply thinking about your body and actually being present to your body. On Day One the golfer was present to his body, and in this state there wasn't a lot of room for interference.

Then on the second day, his focus lessened because his mind did what it usually does and thoughts and judgments began to creep in. There was still a residue of the physical experience of Day One, but the golfer had at this point drifted to being present mostly to the thoughts about his body, not to his body itself. But he was not aware that he had shifted from being in a physical domain to a mixture of mental and physical domains. The difference between be- ing in his body and *thinking* about his body is blurred. This difference is crucial, since it's like the difference between eating the meal and eating the menu.

By Day Three, the only thing left is thought. The golfer is almost completely in his head, remembering, trying hard. There is a lot of doubt and trust is low. Consequently, there may be overtightening but it is unnoticed. It's back to square one with all the accompanying frustration, as most golfers know only too well. From my experience, this is the typical life cycle of a key swing thought.

So examine your own experience. Whether you've played golf for twenty years or just a few, it's likely you've gone through an amazing number of key swing thoughts, each with a life cycle similar to that described above. Yet I would guess that at least part of you is hoping this book will give you another such thought, or perhaps several. It's fascinating that even if the "tried" is not so true, most people still go down the same old path. Why don't we say, "Wait a second! Isn't there anything else? Can I rely on anything other than key swing thoughts?"

Let's start there.

THINKING ABOUT THINKING

If you as a golfer could have only one skill, what would you want it to be? What would be the *most* important skill? I've asked hundreds golf professionals this question and a great deal of them say that the most important skill for golf is "concentration," or "focus." The relationship between concentration and learning is undeniable. I then ask the pros, "If that's so, do you teach concentration?" Almost everyone says no. If I follow this with, "How many of you receive lessons in this important skill?" the answer again is almost always no.

If something is so important, why don't we coach it? Like all of us in our school days, I spent quite a number of years absorbing information, but no one instructed me on how to concentrate, and I never learned how to learn. It was assumed I knew how. Looking back, I see that if I had spent time learning about learning and concentration, my school experience would probably have been much richer and more enjoyable. The same applies to golf and putting. Great feats in putting (or any endeavor) are always achieved in a state of relaxed concentration and mental calm. They rarely, if ever, happen in a state of agitation or dual-mindedness. So the words "concentration," "learning how to learn" and "being calm" have a unique relationship, which I would like to explore before we go to our first exercise.

When I ask students, "When is the only time you can learn?" it becomes quite obvious that the only time is right now. This time. This moment. How often are we in this moment rather than in some projection of the future or in some attempt to remember the past? As we talked about earlier, very few people are actually in this time, present to what's happening right now. One of the first things about learning is to realize that it has a lot to do with being present in this moment. Coaching is, in part, about helping the student recover the sensitivity and the innocence that is required for self-discovery and self-coaching. It's also about bringing them back to this moment, and asking them to let go of the agendas that take them away.

While we're hitting golf shots, there's a lot of stuff that tries to pull us away from being present. Concentration and focus allow us to bring our attention to here and now. There's a litmus test for concentration that I have offered to hundreds of golfers, and I ask you to take it. First, determine where your attention is *before* your putting stroke starts. Take a look. What are you paying attention to? Where is your focus? Whatever it is, note it. Second, determine where your attention is *after* your stroke is finished. Was it on the very same thing, with the same quality, or had it shifted in the mere two seconds that it took to hit the ball?

I've asked this question to hundreds of people and almost no one has ever said, "Where my attention is at the start of the motion is exactly where it is at the end." Most people's attention wanders all over the place but they don't know it, and that's the critical issue. What would it be like to have one focus and keep it all the way to the end, and also to develop the capacity to recognize when you've shifted attention and come back quickly? Great learners aren't always present; they get distracted like everyone else. But they have great comeback ability.

Concentration speaks to our capacity to be present to that which we intend, for as long as we intend. It has a lot to do with curiosity, fascination, intention, courage and letting go of irrelevancies.

I think we can get to the essence of it in this exercise. The goal is to focus on what's real in golf, and there are four things: your body, the ball, the club and the environment, which includes the target. Each of these has physical substance, mass. For the purpose of this exercise we'll call them real. Now pick one, let's say the clubhead. Can you be present to the head of the club from the beginning to the end of the swing? Can you be with it all the way until the movement stops? Now, here's the rub: Odds are you won't be most of the time. But as in the previous exercises, begin to see how you go away—catch your mind doing its thing.

· *Peace of Mind Exploration* ·
Exercise #2a: Concentration
on the Clubhead

(a) Take your putter and assume your normal putting stance,
but with no ball present. As you hold the putter, get a sense of the

head of the club. Take a normal putting stroke and keep your attention on the clubhead, all the way from beginning to end. Notice if your attention shifts. Keep going until you feel your attention is consistently with the clubhead all the way through.

(b) Now do the same exercise but add a ball. Don't worry about putting to a hole or any other target. Simply address the ball, focusing your attention on the head of the club, and putt it, intending to keep your attention on the clubhead until the end of the stroke. Notice what happens, and if the presence of the ball affects your ability to hold your chosen focus.

Two great sources of interference in golf are doubt and fear. When a person is present to what's here now (e.g., the clubhead), if only for the duration of the two seconds it takes to swing, there's no room for doubt and fear to come in. So being present to an area of the swing accomplishes two things: (1) you learn about the thing upon which you are focusing your attention, and (2) you leave no room for doubt, fear or other mental interference to come in.

If you've played this game for fifteen years, you've probably hit at least fifty thousand golf shots. It's likely you haven't been present to one of them from beginning to end, so taking on the challenge of this exercise will be excellent training. It will require you to be intentional about staying present, to notice what takes you away, to let go of what takes you away and to come back to your original intention (e.g., to stay with the clubhead, target, the ball, etc.).

What's truly fascinating, as we've said before, is that when you can have one focus from beginning to end, everything starts to show up. I know it sounds a little funny but it's true.

If you are truly, completely present to one thing, you will start to have awarenesses—feelings and sensitivities—you've never had before. The whole world will start to show up. Strange as it may seem, when you can have one single focus, you can have it all.

However, most people hardly ever achieve a clear, constant focus, since almost everyone leaves their intended focus the moment they touch the ball. I've asked thousands of people if they've experienced the last part of their stroke and almost no one says they have. They have no idea what the putter does after it hits the ball. Yet the most important time in a golf swing is the time when all the feedback comes—the two or three seconds after we've putted the ball. It's when our physical system assesses what happened with our body, the club and the ball. This feedback takes time and requires us to be present to receive it.

• Peace of Mind Exploration •
Exercise #2b: Deepening Concentration

Do the same as in the previous exercise, picking one "real" part of the swing and staying with it through the entire stroke. Try this with your body, the ball or the target. As always, if your attention wanders, simply notice what it does and bring yourself back to your intended focus. It's likely that one of these areas of focus will prove to be the most interesting and enjoyable, and if so, stay with it. Remember that the goal is fascination, not hard work.

These exercises are simple in their intention: to discover the nature of your attention, to develop your capacity to focus, to recognize when you've left your focus and to come back. It's important to be clear about where you leave and when you come back—about when you're there and when you're not.

Given the value of concentration, I've often wondered why I wasn't coached in it in first grade. It is crucial not only in all sports, but in all learning. When someone is completely focused, it's effortless and there's always joy. If you did nothing more than play golf to develop concentration, it would be well worth it.

One more comment about key swing thoughts. These thoughts bring the past into the present, as do all acts of remembering. Concentration in golf is simply being present to something that is real. Key swing thoughts are thoughts, and even though they seem real, they aren't. Although they may appear to contain important information and the obvious goal is to have them improve your game, in the end they become another form of interference.

Chapter Twelve

PEACE OF MIND
EXPLORATION #3:
NARROW FOCUS

You can tell a lot about a culture by its language. Es-kimos, for example, have many different words for snow while we have but one. On the other hand, we have multiple words for vehicles (car, truck, bus, sedan, minivan, etc.) while they undoubtedly have fewer. The reasons are obvious.

Some cultures have many words for concentration, dif-ferentiating between states, levels and intensities, while our culture has but one. Knowing concentration to be an essen-tial ingredient in golf performance, it makes sense to ex-plore its details, and its subtleties. Concentration can have a broad focus or a narrow focus, for example, and in this next exercise we'll explore an extremely narrow one: the focus needed to have the edge of the clubface and the center of the ball meet precisely. The process you'll go through will be excellent training of your concentration and will help develop a sensitivity you can bring to your putter, allowing you to hit the ball in the center of the putter more often. Most people rarely hit putts in the center of the putter face.

• *Peace of Mind Exploration* • *Exercise #3: Narrow Focus*

Take your sand wedge and go out to the putting green with a few balls. Stand 5 or 6 feet from a hole and putt the balls to the hole with the wedge. Notice what kind of focus it takes to hit the very center of the ball with the bottom edge of the blade. If you hit high, the ball will bounce. If you hit low, the ball will jump in the air. The challenge is to hit the ball so that it rolls smoothly to the hole.

One of the best things about this exercise is the instant feedback you receive. If the ball is hit anywhere but center, it will either bounce or jump in the air. As you proceed, notice the sensitivity that's needed in your hands, and the kind of focus that is required. Notice what you have to let go of (thoughts, expectations, etc.). Pay particular attention to the automatic thoughts, the first ones that pop up, some of which will certainly be about how hard and unnatural it is to putt with a wedge. Is it really? Don't let your mind determine that—find out for yourself.

You'll discover that when you can hit a ball solidly with a sand wedge, you will have developed an increased level of concentration. Once this happens, begin to notice what's going on with your body. How much tension resides in it? How do you bend over? What kind of "seeing" is required? You may also find that the length and acceleration of your putting stroke change. Perhaps when you use your regular putter, this new focus and sensitivity will make quite a difference. Also, note the relationship between concentration and peace of mind.

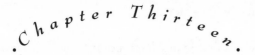

Chapter Thirteen

PEACE OF MIND
EXPLORATION #4:
EXPOSING JUDGMENT

Judgment (def.): *A formal utterance of an authoritative opinion formed by evaluating and comparing.*

When I first began giving golf lessons, I thought "judging" was part of my job description. I assumed I was supposed to judge and evaluate swings, and pass on important information in order to have my students come to a greater understanding of their golf motion. I believed I was paid to deliver judgment, evaluation, information and understanding, thinking these would produce greater performance and more enjoyment. This is what I had seen other golf instructors do. It's what others had told me they did and what I'd read about.

After a few thousand golf lessons, I became very good at this. I was the golf "doctor" who had a great "eye" for the swing and could pinpoint the faults and provide the fixes.

There was only one problem: It didn't work. In a few thousand lessons, nothing really remarkable happened with my students, and my lessons had all become very predictable.

So for the next few thousand lessons, I took the next logical step: I got better at it! I provided different, more finely tuned evaluations and the latest information. I made sure my students knew a lot about "the swing," including putting.

Still nothing happened that could be considered exceptional or even unpredictable. Hour after hour, day after day, week after week, wonderfully motivated people would come to my lesson tee. I would greet them, watch a few swings and launch into my "stuff." The golf "doctor" would perform informational and evaluative surgery. They expected it and I provided it. It was the paradigm we all knew. And it really didn't work. There were no miracles.

I knew there had to be some other possibility, something other than the uninspiring pattern in which I seemed to be stuck. Even through my veneer of resignation, I had a sense that after aeons of human evolution, the final word on learning this sport could not be merely, "Take it down from the inside against a firm left side," or "Keep your head down and don't peek."

I thought about some of the commonplace things that everyone takes for granted but that are really remarkable in their own way. Somehow people have been able to learn to walk, talk, ride a bike and throw a baseball in an efficient way without the type of teaching I was providing. Miracles and extraordinary learning can happen, but how? What was the opening, the access? What is the greatest barrier to learning? Or another way to look at it, what's the difference between a four-year-old learning to ride a bicycle and a thirty-year-old learning to hit a driver? The answer became obvious: judgments. Four-year-olds don't drift out of a physical realm to think about and evaluate their performance against an acceptable model. They are present to—and have permission to be with—what is. Without judgment. They have the freedom to experience the physical activity as is, without the constraints or burden of how it should be. The very thing that I had trained myself for as a teacher, evaluating/comparing students against models of what should be, was the greatest barrier to learning. How ironic.

There was one other realization that emerged as I began to observe judgment in my students and myself. I began to see that the judgments themselves were not fully the problem, because after all, they pop up all the time; they're automatic and part of being human. "Good swing, bad swing, right way, wrong way"—thoughts like these just happen. It was when these judgments stayed hidden—when good/bad/right/wrong weren't seen as judgments—that was the problem. Once we—my students and I—could recognize the judgments as just thoughts—the Voice—and not keep following them down their tunnel, we could come back to the task at hand, which I now defined as expanding awareness and developing self-reliance and self-coaching. So my original conclusion was modified: The greatest barrier to learning is not just judgments but hidden, unrecognized judgments that control present and future actions and put us in some mental drama.

The degree to which hidden judgments interfere with our learning and performance and disrupt our peace of mind is, in my experience, astounding. I urge you to take a look and draw your own conclusions. Here's an exercise to expose hidden judgments, one that can provide a contrast to our usual experience of observing a putt. And here's my new working definition of judgment:

> Judgment (new def.): *An automatic, unauthoritative thought that is past-based, clouds the reality before us and, if hidden, sabotages learning.*

• *Peace of Mind Exploration Exercise #4* • *Exposing Judgments*

Go to the putting green and simply putt balls to a target. Instead of watching the ball once you complete your stroke, watch the actual shadow that the ball makes (not the after-image) on the ground as it rolls. When the ball is touching the ground the shadow will be partial, but if the ball bounces you will see the whole oval shadow. Note what the experience is like when you're simply watching the shadow. We can call that "absence of judgment." Perhaps you're experiencing a state of mild interest or curiosity, or even amazement. Then alternate between watching the ball on a putt and watching the shadow on another putt. This exercise is to distinguish judgment from other states of being.

As you do this exercise, you might be able to experience that when you watched the ball before it may have mostly been in judgment. There was likely very little pure awareness or interest. When you putt and look at the shadow, you may experience something very different; and when you go back to putting and watching the ball, you may notice how hooked you are in evaluation and judgment. When you expose it and see it for what it is, then you have a choice of coming back to the task at hand.

We give many Extraordinary Golf workshops in Japan, and it's always fascinating to see how Japanese experience the different exercises. One group became particularly fascinated with the after-image exercise (Freedom Exercise #1a: The Spot), giving the phantom image a special name: *zanzo*. They felt that the shadow of the ball in this exercise had similar magical qualities and dubbed it "moving zanzo," a name that seems to fit perfectly. It captures the feel of something that, although it has always been there, has a transformational effect when seen for the first time.

So look for moving zanzo, and you may never see a putt the same way again.

PEACE OF MIND EXPLORATIONS SUMMARY

Whenever I hear someone say something to the effect of, "I feel more at peace now than before," it seems as if they've let go of something rather than found or added something. This sense of releasing matches my own experience.

The exercises in this section were about letting go

. . . of the automatic voice in our head;
. . . of the incessant search for key swing thoughts;
. . . of judgments.

What's left underneath all that is a calm, clear presence and a peace of mind that seems like "nothing." I think it's obvious that "nothing" can help your putting.

Part Three

SELF-COACHING
EXPLORATIONS

PREFACE: THE NATURE OF REALITY

The main theme of this book is awareness. Awareness is connected with your relationship to reality. Of course, the whole notion of "reality" is a subject in itself, so let me just give a quick overview of what I mean by this relationship.

Consider the following drawing:

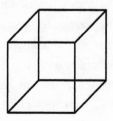

If you were to ask someone what this is, they would say a cube. But a real cube, of course, is a three-dimensional object. This drawing is actually just twelve lines on a piece of paper. The lines are arranged in such a way that we create the image of a three-dimensional object in our minds, and so we "see" a cube. We use the same word to refer to both "realities," but this doesn't cause a problem in normal circumstances since we can easily integrate the two.

Problems arise when there are big gaps between the two: between a physical reality and the image, or story, we create about it. We all know of people who have this problem to the extent that it is difficult for them to function normally—those whose stories about people following them or persecuting them have no basis in the real world. Yet what about the supposed "normal" people, such as the rest of us? The assumption is that our perception of reality is "real," but is this truly the case? Not always, as my life experience has shown me, and certainly not always in golf. My earlier account of my immediate "explanations" of my mishit shots is but one example of many.

The truth is what philosophers and mystics have been saying all along: Our personal reality is entirely subjective, created by us to give meaning to what we experience around us. The closer these internal creations match what is actually happening, the better we function in the world and the more successful we're likely to be at whatever we try to do. But since the only way we can connect with this "outside" reality is through our inner experience, for us the words "reality" and "inner experience" are one and the same. Therefore when I speak of "awareness of what's happening" in golf, I mean paying attention to our experience and the differences in that experience from stroke to stroke, or swing to swing.

Given all this, what we're after in self-coaching is threefold:

1. To have the things that are critically important but not on our radar screen begin to hit the radar screen. In other words, there are many areas that we do not experience in our swing and therefore we do not know what's occurring in them. Let's call them "blind spots." The goal is to start filling in those areas with the light of awareness so they are blind no longer.

2. To be able to experience the variations within those blind areas and start experiencing how those variations create different outcomes.

3. To start bridging the gap between what we think is happening and what is actually happening. In other words, moving closer to the point where the reality of what we experience matches the reality a camera would show.

The following exercises are designed to accomplish the above.

SELF-COACHING
EXPLORATION #1:
REALITY CHECK

What gives you more joy in life, learning or performance? If I had to bet on how most people would answer that question, I'd say most would pick performance: when they hit a great golf shot, or scored the winning basket, or got an A on a test, etc. There's no denying that many of our fondest memories are of times when we performed well.

We live in a culture that holds up performance as the highest goal, not only in sports but also in business. Extraordinary Golf has worked with many companies, some of which considered themselves to be "learning organizations." Yet I've never worked with an organization as dedicated to a culture of learning as it was to our current culture of performance. If there were truly a learning culture, questions such as "What are you learning?" would be common, yet I've rarely heard them. Learning for the simple joy of learning is not often seen.

I'm not trying to belittle performance. Like anyone, I, too, love to perform well. The point I want to make is that tomorrow's performance depends on today's learning. But our current learning culture is very weak. It sees learning as a necessary step on the road to performance, something to move through, to get done with, rather than something to enjoy. Not only are we not trained in how to learn, if we acknowledge that we need to learn it can sometimes work against us. For example, if people in business ask to be coached, they are often seen as weak or "less than" they should be. There is great pressure to look as if we know what we're doing, or at least know how to find out what to do. We're embarrassed to be seen as not knowing so we pretend that we know. Underneath it all is a given assumption that we know how to learn, and therefore if we don't learn it's our own fault.

With this background, it's difficult to become fine learners. And if there's no real learning taking place today, then it's illogical to assume that tomorrow's performance will be any different from today's.

So how can we learn how to learn with regard to our putting, and the rest of our golf game? All the exercises up to this point have been designed to get us on this path, and it doesn't hurt to use appropriate technology to help us along as well. This next series of exercises uses video of your putting stance and stroke. You'll need a video camera, preferably with slow-motion and stop-action capabilities in the playback (or a digital camera with video capability); and a partner (or a tripod), with the filming taking place on the practice green as you are putting to a hole about 10 feet away. If you don't currently have access to a video camera but think you might at some future time (a teaching pro's camera, for instance), you can skip to the next section ("Watching the Video to Produce a Breakthrough"). Reading it can offer a new way of seeing.

Here are the three perspectives from which the videos should be taken:

1. From behind the person putting, far enough to get the entire scene in view, including the full body (from head to ball), the line of the putt, and

VIDEO POSITION I: FROM BEHIND

the hole in the distance (leave the flagstick in).
You should be able to see the person's eyes, shoulders and hips in this shot.

2. From a shorter distance behind the person putting, slightly above ground level. We should see a close-up of the putter and ball, with the line of the ball visible and the hole in the background. Again, leave the pin in so that some of it appears in the shot; this will provide a marker from which you will be able to see how the putter comes back and forth.

VIDEO POSITION 2:
CLOSER UP FROM BEHIND

3. From the side (relative to the direction of the putt), in a full-body shot of the front of the person putting. The hole should not be seen, just the golfer's body, from head down to the ball.

VIDEO POSITION 3: FROM THE SIDE

· *Self-Coaching Exploration Exercise #1* · *Reality Check*

(a) With a partner (or a tripod), use a video camera (or a digital camera with video capability) to film your putting stroke from the three perspectives outlined and illustrated above: (1) from behind, full-body shot; (2) from behind, close-up; (3) from the side, full-body. Film several putts (about 20 feet) from each angle.

(b) Review the videos, looking not for what's wrong but for what surprises you—the things you didn't know were happen-

ing. Notice the difference between what you thought was the reality of your putting stroke versus what the camera reveals.

This is the easy part—filming ourselves. But for most people it's not so easy to watch ourselves on film. How we view and review our videos will determine how much we learn from them, so let's learn about this learning process.

WATCHING THE VIDEO TO
PRODUCE A BREAKTHROUGH

You'll likely watch the video playback hoping that it looks good, according to the standard you hold. You won't want to see anything that you think is not good or wrong. We film all the students in our Extraordinary Golf programs, and for me it's an immensely exciting time because I imagine the possibility of great learning coming out of the session. But I notice that in the beginning most people are embarrassed to see their videos to the point where they'd rather skip the whole thing. It's the old head-in-the-sand approach of, "I don't want to see what's really going on, I just want to be fixed and get better." Like everyone in our culture, the students have been indoctrinated into the previously mentioned learning paradigm of "let's swallow this bitter pill of embarrassment and get on with it."

The normal way is to look for what's wrong and then try to make it better. If you're more golf-savvy than most, you'll have a wealth of information against which to measure your video, and you'll apply a standard of right and wrong that is very subtle and extensive. But this would still be the same paradigm of "there's something wrong with my motion and I need to get it fixed." This type of looking is only ordinary, no matter how much information you have. Let's follow the premise of the previous exercise: that all great learning starts with a new point of view. This tells us that if we want a real breakthrough, we need to look at the video with "new eyes."

So instead of the automatic looking for what's wrong, look for what *surprises* you.

Can you let go of the judgments that will automatically come up and simply watch for what's being revealed? What do you see that you didn't know was happening? What are you seeing that you didn't sense? Can curiosity replace judgment?

The following are places to begin looking. Remember that the goal is not judgment but fascination. Look for what surprises you, for what you hadn't experienced.

In camera angle #1 (behind, full-body):

- Where is your body actually pointing? Where are the shoulders pointing? Hips? Forearms? Feet?
- Are your eyes over the ball? Inside? Outside? How is the angle of your spine?
- How does the putter come back and forth related to the target? How is the putter face pointed at the hole at the beginning of the stroke? Left? Right?

In camera angle #2 (behind, close-up):

- Can you see where the blade hits the ball? Is it high or low? Is it on the toe or the heel? If there's a line on the top of the putter that marks the sweet spot, can you see whether the putter hits in the center or not?

In camera angle #3 (side, full-body):

- Is the shaft of the putter at the angle you thought it was? Is it tilted forward? Backward?
- Where is the ball played in your stance in relation to your head? On the right ear? Left ear? Nose?
- How about the tilt of your shoulders? What's the reality of that?
- Can you see your face? Is it buried down? Is your head up?
- Are the back and forward swings of comparable lengths or different?
- Do you accelerate through the ball or slow down?

Forget where you think everything should be, according to the latest putting theories. Simply find out where you are right now. If you're looking from this perspective, viewing the video should not occur to you as an information overload. If it does, then take a look at what you're doing with what you're seeing—you've probably slipped into a mode of evaluation, relating all this back to the theories I mentioned earlier.

If your experience is anything like mine, watching videos from this new point of view makes them immensely fascinating. There's so much to see! Once you are able to let go of judgments—a continuous process of comparing what you see to a remembered model—it turns what could be an unpleasant, embarrassing experience into something enjoyable and energizing. Have your observations matched what you imagined your putting stroke would look like? Have you had many surprises? As always, inaccurate putters encounter more surprises than more accurate putters. Excellent putters have few surprises—their sense of the reality of what's happening is highly accurate—whereas less proficient putters' sense of reality is off to a high degree. It's always the case.

The argument is easily made that the only way one develops in this game is to get a greater sense of what's actually happening. I probably play better golf than most of the people I coach for one simple reason: I sense more accurately what's happening during the swing than they do. My blind spots are fewer and smaller—period. That's what makes a better golfer. Every one of us has the capability for that depth of awareness.

KNOWING ABOUT "KNOWING"

Reiterating what we said earlier about "knowing" could have some value here. Visually perceiving something about your swing is a first step, but seeing something happening on video doesn't mean you *know* what's happening. In the typical usage of the word, "knowing" means that you've received information about something. But we have a different meaning for this word in Extraordinary Golf. We define "knowing" as having had a direct experience of something *in the moment* that it occurs. This type of knowing is distinct from information. Information is no longer necessary once you have had the experience of something.

Increasing your awareness is the only thing that will make a real difference, and this has little to do with information. As you have seen, the exercises in this book are all about getting you out of your head (information) and into your body (experience). The video clips are tremendous sources of information that will be valuable only to the extent that you can successfully make the transition to experience.

So let's say you find several areas in the video that surprise you. When you go back to the green, can you simply experience them as they are? Can you let go of trying to alter them for now? Can you develop fascination in the process of experiencing what's going on, instead of acting out the addiction of "I have to change it because it's embarrassing not to do it right"? For instance, if you notice that your shoulders are in an open position on the video, can you experience their openness without trying to change them? Can there be curiosity in the discovery? If you saw that your putter face was closed (or open), can you simply begin to observe how it is? Can you give yourself permission to sense it rather than trying to change it? When it isn't about right or wrong, or being embarrassed, most people experience a lot more joy in the process of learning.

THE SOURCE OF CHANGE

Here's another fundamental premise of Extraordinary Golf, one also validated by thousands of golf lessons and workshops:

> *Attempting to change things you haven't experienced ensures that they won't change.*

The primary source of failure of most golf teaching is that people attempt to change things they have not experienced, which is impossible to do. Without experience, students don't know where they're starting from, and when they return to an old pattern of motion, they don't know they've come back to it. Is there any wonder why the results of this approach are usually less than satisfying?

After thirty years of coaching, I would say that I have observed one consistent miracle in golf, and it is this: Awareness is curative. When a person becomes aware of a blind spot (like open shoulders) by simply experiencing or observing it without judgment, a natural change takes place, and in that moment a more efficient motion begins to emerge. Now back to the video . . .

The goal of this exercise is to catch yourself in the act of doing what you're doing. I can promise you that if you begin to tune in to areas that surprise you in the video, there will be some—maybe only just one—that will be a critical variable. It may be where the ball is hit on the blade, or where the putter face is pointing or how much movement there is before or during the striking of the ball. You will find one that will make a difference if you can simply experience it. That's what we're looking for in this exercise.

Once you can sense where you are, no matter what area of the swing you focus on, your body will naturally explore new possibilities. It's inevitable. A curiosity will emerge and a natural learning will take place: You know where you are, you know (experience) a new possibility and you experience the difference. That's learning. You don't have to worry about choosing a more efficient motion or position: your body will choose.

SELF-COACHING
EXPLORATION #2:
DISTINGUISHING

There's more to experience than just experience. As I said in an earlier exercise, there is the relationship of experience to reality and how it can grow closer to "camera reality" over time. Experience alone is not the teacher. There's another word we can use that gets to the heart of learning, and that is "distinguishing." Within the experience one is able to distinguish—notice more and more subtle differences—and get closer to reality.

Let me illustrate the difference between the two. A few years out of college I joined the Peace Corps and spent two years as a teacher in Ghana, West Africa. As in much of Africa, there are a great many different ethnic tribes in Ghana, and I lived near six of them. My initial experience was that all Ghanaian tribes were the same and I couldn't tell them apart. So having been there one month, it would have been accurate, according to my personal experience, for me to state that the tribes of Ghana could not be differentiated from one another. Yet a few months later I could identify all six tribes as easily as I can people in the U.S. They were so uniquely different that it was mind-boggling that I could ever have seen them as being alike.

At that point I hadn't significantly changed, the tribal situation hadn't changed, yet something different had occurred with me. My first few months had been clouded with the typical fears and anxieties of culture shock, and this interfered with my perception. Over time I settled in, the shock (and interference) lessened and I was able to pay closer attention to the people around me. Subtleties emerged and I became able to "distinguish."

Now, let me put this in terms of putting, specifically as it relates to reading greens. This is an example of a scenario I've experienced many times.

I'm playing golf with an amateur partner, and we read a putt together. I ask him, "What do you see in terms of the break?" He says that he thinks it will break 6 inches right to left. It looks to me like it will break a lot more than that but I say, "Let's see. I'll give it a shot." I then point *2 feet* right and putt along that line. The putt goes in, and my partner says, "See, six inches outside the right lip was perfect."

What's interesting is that the putt broke 2 feet, but all he saw were 6 inches. His *experience* was that the putt broke 6 inches, so when he left the putting green he took away a reality of a 6-inch break when the physical reality was 2 feet. It seems mysterious, yet it happens all the time.

At almost all Extraordinary Golf programs there is a point where we get all the students in a group behind a putt with some break to it. We ask them to describe how much the putt breaks. We place tees to the side of the hole to represent their estimates: 3, 4, 12 inches, etc. Then I putt a ball and ask them to describe what they saw of the break. Out of twelve people, for example, typically only one person describes it accurately. The others almost always estimate less than the full amount of the break. By "full amount" I mean the distance from the point farthest from the side of the hole to the hole itself.

After putting three more, I again ask the students what they see. Usually eleven of the twelve increase their break a bit. If it was 3 inches, the person says 6. If it was 6, the person says 8. Now if the putt actually breaks 2 feet, almost no one will report accurately on the break, even after having seen at least three putts from that distance. Rarely does anyone see reality, and this has been proven not just by my experience but by many studies as well. One of these studies recommends that people putt to twice the break they read. This suggestion may be a reasonable coping method, but it does nothing toward improving your perception of reality or developing trust in yourself and your abilities. There are other possibilities.

BLIND JUDGMENT WHEN READING GREENS

In a workshop we draw a line in chalk on the green from the ball to the maximum break point—say 2 feet to the side of the cup. I then step up and putt balls down the line. At some point the ball will leave the line and curve toward the hole. Typically, almost everyone says, "Wow! I didn't see that!"

Why not? Why haven't they seen it after repeated demonstrations? Where have they been that they didn't see that all the balls broke 2 feet? We ask people what they did see when they looked and they usually report seeing something like "good putt, bad putt." So blinded by this judgment, they miss an entire segment of the break. They miss seeing what really happens.

As we've said before, the greatest barrier to learning is judgment. It's also the greatest barrier to reading greens. What would it be like to let go of judgment and wake up to seeing the whole thing? To really see how the putt starts, where it breaks and how much it breaks? In our golf program, we might chalk off nine holes on a putting green to clearly illustrate the breaks, which can range from 6 inches to 8 feet or more. This helps students start moving their experiential reality more toward the reality of the green.

So getting back to my earlier comment about distinguishing versus experiencing . . .

Every time a person putts, there is some experience, but the experience may have little similarity to what really happens. Most people don't start their putts on the line they intend. If they imagine a 6-inch break in a putt—that in reality curves 2 feet from right to left—they'll aim the putt approximately 6 inches to the right of the cup and push it farther right during the stroke. Brilliantly, their body has learned to accommodate for the difference by modifying the stroke. On some level, their body knows what works better. What's most interesting is that they don't know they pushed it and actually think they hit it 6 inches to the right of the hole. In order to catch what really happens, they need to distinguish *seeing* from merely *looking*.

You don't need to set down chalk lines to reap the benefit of seeing. Here's an exercise that can help:

• *Self-Coaching Exploration Exercise #2* • *Reading Greens*

Go to the practice green and find putts that have varying amounts of break. Instead of putting, first simply roll balls toward the holes with your hand. Watch the entire length of the break. When you are aware of the quality of attention needed to see accurately, start putting and notice if the quality of your attention—your seeing—changes with the putter in hand.

Great green readers aren't people who just have some knack for it. They are people who have trained themselves in seeing and are "awake" on the putting green. On some level they have developed the ability to see objectively, outside of good/bad, tough/easy, and they use every opportunity to read the green. This is in contrast to the typical player, as in the following example.

A foursome arrives near the green on a particular hole. Two players are already on the green, and they wait while the other two chip up. Then the two players farthest from the hole putt. It's now the third person's turn to putt, and he has had the advantage of seeing two chips and two putts. But he stood there all that time without taking in any of the information the green revealed when a ball landed or rolled on it. And now he wonders as he eyes his putt, "How much does it break?"

Great green readers, on the other hand, are like cats watching a gopher hole. They are alert, awake, fascinated. They watch everybody's chip, everybody's putt. They even look at how balls roll on the green from 100 yards. They see it all. They see the whole green and get a sense of it even as they walk toward it. They have an ongoing curiosity about what's happening.

Reading greens requires a finely developed awareness. Most of the golf professionals you see on TV awakened to this kind of seeing at an early age and have continued to develop it whenever possible. Most amateurs stand beside the green and are only mildly observant. If you can begin to see clearly what's going on, of course you'll learn to read greens. All that we've talked about up to this point—being able to distinguish the reality of your body, club and target, to observe without judgment, to have a sense of freedom, to be able to let go and trust yourself—all of that is wonderful. But this all rests on a foundation of being able to see what is actually happening on the greens.

So, wake up! It's a full-time job to stay asleep and we're so often asleep in golf. Yet everyone says that the most enjoyable moments of their lives are the moments when they are awake, here, in the moment. Not in some story, judgment or evaluation. Not in the past. Not in the future, but seeing what is really happening here and now.

Can you be intrigued enough to peel away your misperceptions and peer into what is actually happening? I have no interest in making you feel that you should go out and practice reading greens. My intention is for you to become so fascinated and passionate about the process that you can't stay away.

SELF-COACHING
EXPLORATION #3: IS THE
PRACTICE STROKE ENOUGH?

My father is ninety years old and I've played golf with him for forty-eight years, ever since he first carried me around the course as a toddler and let me putt on a few holes. Some years ago Dad requested that I coach him on his putting game, commenting that his control of distance had been erratic.

During a round we played together, I observed both his practice and actual putting strokes. On a 30-foot putt his practice stroke seemed to have enough power to roll 15 feet, 20 at the most. Applying the same stroke to his actual putt would have left him continually short, but his body—his inner wisdom—was brilliant. Without being conscious of it, he compensated for the lack of power with a move that enabled him to make up the difference. The backswing of his putting stroke matched that of his practice stroke, but just before his putter reached the ball he'd jab at it and the ball would roll close to 30 feet.

The jab was his body's attempt to get the ball to the hole when his swing lacked the power. But this type of jerky motion is tough to replicate consistently, so sometimes the ball would go 35 feet, sometimes 25, sometimes less. This compensatory move exhibited itself at every level of his putting stroke, from the shortest to the longest putts. If Dad putted a 5-footer, his practice stroke had energy to roll the ball approximately 3 feet.

The interesting part is that Dad's personal reality was that his practice stroke was sufficient for the distance. He had no sense that his practice and actual putting strokes differed so much. The gap between his reality and the camera's reality was large. The coaching approach was therefore simple: Could we create an exercise that would bring Dad's experience closer to reality?

So we started our work together. I simply asked him to make practice strokes that he thought were appropriate to his target 20 feet away. After a few strokes, I asked him if he thought the practice stroke was the right amount. He said he did. Once again, I could see that the stroke lacked the energy to propel the ball 20 feet although he believed it did. We needed to create something that would allow him to see his stroke anew. Here's the exercise we engaged in that day, one that we've subsequently used with many students, since there's a little of Dad's putting stroke in many of us.

• Self-Coaching Exploration Exercise #3a •
Is the Practice Stroke Enough?

(a) Find a partner and go to the putting green with a supply of balls. Set up about 20 feet away from a hole and find a practice stroke you think is appropriate for that distance. Keep this same stroke continuously going back and forth, close enough to the ground that it would hit a ball solidly. Then close your eyes.

(b) Taking care not to touch your putter while it is moving, your partner occasionally places balls where the ball would normally lie. With your eyes closed, you will occasionally hit balls when they've been placed. Don't let the experience of ball impact stop you, just keep your eyes closed and keep the stroke going back and forth. (After a few ball placements, your partner will have found the spot to place the ball that allows you to hit it solidly, even with your eyes closed.) After hitting a dozen or so balls, open your eyes and notice whether the balls ended up where you thought they would.

HOLDING THE BALL ABOVE   PLACING THE BALL

Are the balls close to your target? They probably aren't. Most nonprofessional golfers exhibit practice swings with too little or too much power for their target, but they don't know it and there's no reality check for it. To them, like my dad, it seems as though the stroke is right on.

Many fascinating things occur during this exercise, and there are variations on the basic theme. In a program setting, for instance, if the coaches see that a student putts the ball consistently short of the target, we ask them to open their eyes on the last putt. This last putt is interesting because most likely the student will unconsciously alter their stroke just before impact in order to make the ball reach the hole. In fact, they'll likely believe that their stroke was sufficient, despite having putted eleven out of the twelve balls short with the same essential backstroke. At that point, the added motion (which could be a flinch, jab, push, etc.) is unknown to them, outside their reality/experience. This change in the stroke is their body's brilliant way of getting the ball to the intended target. But for the body to adapt each single stroke perfectly and accurately each time is difficult, particularly with interference. And so the compensation isn't consistent. I suggest that you start watching great putters. They tend to make a practice stroke that's appropriate to the distance to the target, and they replicate the stroke when they hit the ball. Their practice stroke is a true "practice" of the actual putting event.

So how can you start to develop the appropriate stroke that great putters exhibit? The path to this development starts with becoming aware that you are modifying your stroke when putting the ball.

Here's how my father began to experience what he added to his putting stroke. I first said to him, "Dad, keep taking a practice stroke and I'll tell you when I see that the stroke you're making is about the right amount to get to the hole." Since his stroke had typically been too short, I encouraged him to let go and take a longer, more powerful one. When I felt he had made a stroke appropriate to the distance to the hole, I said, "That's the right amount." He immediately responded with, "Really? I think that would hit it twice as far!" I asked him to withhold judgment while we continued our exploration.

I then asked Dad to swing back and forth with his eyes closed using this new, longer stroke, and I occasionally placed a ball in front of him. Time after time, the balls went the right distance—the stroke was indeed appropriate. Then, with the putting motion continuing, I asked him to open his eyes and I placed a ball that he could hit with open eyes. On this stroke he reintroduced his jabbing motion and the ball rolled 10 feet past the hole. He exclaimed, "See! That's too much stroke for the distance." He had added the familiar little jab to the stroke but hadn't experienced it yet. We had more work to do! But we had definitely made progress, since it started dawning on Dad that the putts with eyes closed went the right distance and the ones with eyes open went longer. He was confused but intrigued.

Once again we went through the eyes-closed to eyes-open progression. But this time I asked Dad to pay particular attention to his forearms and hands and notice if anything changed when he opened his eyes. It took approximately fifteen minutes of work before Dad could experience the muscular sensation of the jab in his hands. When he finally felt it for the first time he exclaimed, "I can't believe I've been doing that all these years!" A blind spot had finally hit the radar screen!

Dad also began to experience variations in the jab: sometimes it was a lot, sometimes a little and finally sometimes none at all—just like the practice stroke. The annoyance of finding out that he had a jab motion turned into curiosity about how much he jabbed, about when (in his downswing) the jab would start and about what muscles were contributing to it. I had Dad close his eyes and take practice strokes again so he could discern that there was no jab motion in them at all. His quality of attention to his arm and hand muscles was now high enough for him to feel their tension or lack of it.

• *Self-Coaching Exploration Exercise #3b* • *Interference in the Stroke*

(a) With the same partner and setup, take continuous practice strokes with eyes open until your partner determines that they are appropriate for the target (a hole about 20 feet away). Continue this same stroke and close your eyes.

(b) In the same way as before, your partner occasionally places balls for you to hit. After you hit a few, your partner tells you to open your eyes and places a ball down. Putt this last ball with eyes open and notice if there is any difference in your stroke. Repeat this sequence to highlight any changes caused by the presence of the ball.

SELF-RELIANCE

Dad started the process of coaching himself when he could fully experience the difference between the two motions. This happened in three phases:

1. He discerned where he was, his starting point. He shed the light of awareness on his blind spot and began to notice what had always been there: his jabbing motion at the ball.
2. Once he was no longer "blind," he was able to explore a new possibility: a stroke truly appropriate to the target.
3. After a short time he could experience the difference between the two—without need of a coach. His body sensed that it didn't need the additional motion of the jab.

Our putting stroke is a miniature version of our other swings, including chipping, pitching and the full swing. I make the same assertion with our practice swings: Our putting practice stroke is a miniature version of our chipping, pitching and full practice swings. The changing of this practice swing when a ball is present, as in my father's case, is also the same in all the swings. We've all seen golfers on the tee take practice swings that show ease and grace, only to see the same golfer with a jabbing, off-balance motion ten seconds later when they hit the ball. The awareness of this alteration is as helpful in all the swings as it is in putting. Since it is easiest to first discern it in putting, an excellent path to improvement is to start this awareness in the putting stroke and develop it in the full swing via chipping and pitching.

One of the underpinnings of developing awareness is "Don't swing any faster—or farther—than you can experience it." The putting practice stroke is a good place to begin to build that foundation of experience. It is the slowest, smallest motion we do in golf and is the easiest place to start building a base of awareness.

INTERLUDE:
GOALS AND VISIONS

For many years, I never set goals. I went through sixteen years of school, played many sports, entered hundreds of golf tournaments, gave thousands of lessons . . . and had no goals. My mind kept saying to me, "There's something wrong about the way I am going about my life." I was thirty years old, very successful in my profession, and yet I felt I should have goals.

A goal is an outcome that will come to completion at a future time, such as: getting a 3.5 grade point average, shooting even par for a tournament or giving 2,500 golf lessons in one year. I could have set these goals and it's possible that this goal setting could have affected the outcome. So why didn't I set them? Was I lazy? Afraid of failure? Success? Accountability?

Many years ago, a coach asked me the question, "What is the purpose for your life?" I said that I didn't know. And just like the coach I wrote about at the beginning of this book, he said, "Maybe you should take a look." Up to that point, I was following, reacting and replicating what I thought I should do according to some societal notion.

I began to look at the world through the lens of the question "What's my purpose?" instead of "What are my goals?" and the world showed up differently. Large questions are much more powerful than someone else's answers.

I saw how grateful and excited I became when a coach created an environment where I could discover my own capabilities and assets, and express them in the world. It occurred to me what a wonderful life it would be to be able to provide that for others—to have people discover their own unique extraordinary nature.

This purpose I chose didn't have to be limited to golf programs. I could be "on purpose" when I am with my family and friends, or even while standing in line at a grocery store. Purpose is timeless and can be "achieved" in every moment in life. A purpose gives us a way to be in this moment and every moment. It's the context that holds all the content. Goals exist in time (the future), and if they don't fall out of a larger purpose, they usually build up stress, fear and doubt.

Let's say my goal is to shoot 72, even par. Do I worry about the outcome during the entire four-hour round? Without a purpose, a deeper vision, I probably do. Now suppose I create the following purpose: to be a person who swings and plays with freedom. I can be connected with this purpose at every moment and with every shot, and the game can now become noticing the freedom and the interference to that freedom. The interference, which I can learn from, is also a partner in my connection to my purpose.

We live in a society where goals and vision are often seen as the same thing. A young pro may come for a lesson and the dialogue could go something like this:

ME: What would you like?

PRO: To be the top player in the Northern California Section.

ME: For what purpose?

PRO: To be the best I can be.

ME: For what purpose?

PRO: I don't get what you're asking.

ME: Why would you take on this quest? What's your vision, your purpose? What's the intention behind it all?

PRO: I'm not sure. . . .

ME: Let's say you become the top player, your stroke average is 70 for the year. Your friends say, "Wow, aren't you something!" And your name gets printed in the newspapers. . . . Is that it? That's all fine but is it worth the hundreds of hours that it will take to achieve? Is that all that turns you on, or is there something more?

PRO: I'd like to consider that for a while.

I remember during one of our programs a student turned to me and said, "In my life, I've found that the context is decisive but that the content is not such a big deal." I understood what he was saying. When the purpose (context) is clear, the goals (content) will flow naturally and will also be clear.

If we keep our eye on the larger purpose, what will emerge are goals that are naturally consistent with it.

Chapter Seventeen

SELF-COACHING
EXPLORATION #4:
THE BLIND WALK

I f you've played golf for a while you've likely noticed that most players either leave putts short of the cup or barely reach the hole, and that their putting stroke is often very tentative. As we have seen, this hesitancy is usually the result of self-interference. Throughout the book, we've looked at the source of this doubt, fear and overtightening with an intent to explore new possibilities.

THE BLIND WALK
In the following exercise, it's possible to distinguish how a goal untethered to a larger vision, a purpose, can generate

fear and doubt. And how a goal connected to a purpose can allow for an entirely different outcome related to that goal.

• *Self-Coaching Exploration Exercise #4a* • *The Blind Walk*

(a) Go to a hole on the practice green and remove the flagstick. Also clear anything else from the vicinity of the hole and anything in your path. Stand approximately 20 feet from the hole and get into your putting stance. While you are in this putting stance, look at the hole as you would if you were to putt. Then, from that position, close your eyes and turn the putter upside down, holding the clubhead in your hand with the grip pointing downward (like a walking stick). Turn and start walking toward the hole with the intent to place the tip of the grip in the hole. Gently put the putter down where you think the cup is and then open your eyes. Notice where the hole is relative to where you thought it was.

THE BLIND WALK

(b) Repeat this sequence from different distances. Don't go back to the same starting point. Keep the distances longer than 10 feet for a while. Do not count your steps; do not use your memory. Just see if you can sense/perceive where the hole is. And begin to notice if there's a pattern. Do you tend to place the putter down short of the hole? Left? Right? Long?

I've been doing this exercise with golfers for more than twenty-five years. At the end of their walk, most put their putters down short of the hole (about 80 percent) and walk tentatively, especially as they near the goal. Students often say that their walk reminds them of their stroke, which is cautious, barely getting the ball to the hole. Can accuracy and confidence be a function of perception? And why does getting nearer the hole increase the doubt?

Let's start with where you look when you look at the hole. Most people usually look from the ball to the hole, reading the break and the slope. That's about all they see. How many people actually look beyond the hole, to the back of the green? To the far horizon? To most of us, the hole is perceived as the end of what we see—it becomes the edge of the "known" area. Whatever is beyond that is perceived as unknown. When a goal sits alone at the edge of a known area, we approach it with caution, doubt and fear. It's natural that when we approach the unknown, we react this way. If you watch people in this blind walking exercise, you'll see that they start off toward the hole with a normal, confident walk. About halfway there they slow down, and during the last part they look tentative and unsure, like someone approaching a cliff.

It isn't that the hole itself frightens us; it's the fact that it is the end of the known area. We don't tend to walk boldly into the unknown—we tread cautiously.

The point here is not to manufacture confidence or aggressiveness. This only leads to forced behavior, as is often seen in scramble tournaments, for example, when three partners have missed a putt and it's the last person's turn. In this situation someone usually reminds the last putter not to leave it short. What often happens is that this person then manufactures a stroke, hits it very long and says, "At least I wasn't short." With the hole as the end of something, a person does not become bold naturally.

• *Self-Coaching Exploration Exercise #4b* • *The Blind Walk—A Shift in Perception*

Can you begin to see the hole as the middle of things? Can you begin to see the hole as part of a "whole"? Even while you are connected to the goal, can you stay connected to the wider vision? Start seeing the area in front of and behind the hole, so that the entire area around the hole becomes known and the hole becomes the middle of this known area. Take blind walks from different distances with this new way of looking.

If you start looking at and really seeing the hole this way, you may begin to notice that your body relaxes. And when you walk toward the hole in the blind walk exercise your pace becomes normal, since you are walking into the middle of a known area. I've observed that after a while in this exercise, people end up closer to the hole and have a greater sense of its location.

As you take this walk from many different distances and directions, you'll be amazed at how you can begin to trust your sense of where the hole is. Your experience of reality will become more accurate, closer to physical reality. Without trying, your putting will develop, and it will develop naturally because of the new way you see, not because you remembered formulas to compensate for what you're not seeing.

PRIMARY SHIFT

With this exercise in mind, I'd like to offer this fundamental premise from our Extraordinary Golf program: Our actions are a function of the way we see the world. In other words, our perspective—our point of view—determines our actions, not the other way around. This insight completely changes the strategy for improving putting, or any action that we do. In the typical coaching situation, we try to change actions by working on the actions themselves, without acknowledging or trying to alter the basic point of view. Typically, it takes a long time to get results and the success rate is not very high. This is a source of great frustration to golfers and golf coaches alike, yet there is no mystery why things happen this way. If point of view determines actions, then the only way to significantly shift actions is to shift the point of view. If the way we see the world stays the same, the actions will stay the same. This is one of the key insights of Extraordinary Golf, one that I see validated every day.

In this exercise, we observe that students do not have a good sense of the distance to the hole, so instead of simply working on their putting stroke (encouraging them to hit it longer, etc.), we work on the way they see the "world." Perceiving the hole as the center of something rather than at the edge of something is a fundamental shift in point of view. With this new perspective their actions—their putts—shift naturally. Having done this blind walk exercise with great putters, I've observed that they tend to place their putter very close to the hole from almost any distance. They tend to see the green in a more "hole"-istic way, which naturally gives rise to trust, confidence and accuracy.

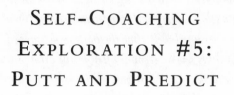

SELF-COACHING
EXPLORATION #5:
PUTT AND PREDICT

This is the litmus test for the previous exercises. Now that you've worked on experiencing differences in your body and the club, and waking up on the green, you can see how your new awareness plays out in reality.

• *Self-Coaching Exploration Exercise #5a* •
Putt and Predict Direction

Take the pin out of a hole and put a small cloth (a handkerchief or a washcloth) in the cup. Have the cloth line the cup in such a way that if the ball were to go in, the cloth would muffle the noise so you wouldn't hear it. Set up about 10 feet away, in a spot where you have a straight putt (no break). Putt balls from this distance with your eyes closed. Can you predict where the balls stop relative to the cup without seeing them? Then experiment with a variety of distances and curves (breaks). Don't open your eyes until well after the balls have stopped. Remember that it takes several seconds after you've hit a putt to process all the feedback. In the first part of the exercise, simply predict whether the balls end up left, right or straight at the hole.

You'll need to tune in to the putter face, your body and the target in order to predict accurately. It's possible to develop your senses to a point where you don't need a sound or a visual confirmation to tell you if the ball is in the hole. As your predictions grow in accuracy, so will your putts. It just happens: Awareness is developmental.

Once you've worked with predicting left or right, you can begin to add a sense of distance.

• *Self-Coaching Exploration Exercise #5b* • *Putt and Predict Distance*

With the hole still muffled, place markers at one-foot increments in front of and behind the hole, and several feet to the side. Again putt balls with your eyes closed, this time guessing distance as well as line, using the markers as reference. Try to visualize the full path of the ball before you open your eyes. Can you sense not only where the ball ends up but also when and how it gets there?

Putting in its simplest form is awareness of distance and direction. This exercise gives an excellent readout of your current state of awareness. It works best if it does not become just another performance game of "good if my prediction is close, bad if it is far off." Can it be a learning exercise instead?

When really fine putters do this exercise, they can predict to a degree that would stun amateur golfers. For instance, when a great putter hits a 20-footer, the prediction may be as specific as "about four inches right and six inches long," with the reality being amazingly close to that. This is an indication of a highly developed awareness, one that could possibly be awakened in all of us.

INTERLUDE:
THE EVER-PRESENT FUTURE

I n chapter 4, I talked about how being present can transform both learning and performance. It's undeniable
that we human beings spend a lot of time thinking about
the past and the future. This time greatly influences the
quality of our lives and that of our internal experience.
Here's how it plays out in golf.

There is an internal experience going on with each of us
as we're about to hit a shot. This experience can range from
confusion to clarity, fear to joy, frustration to gratitude,
doubt to trust, or to a multitude of other possibilities. Have
you ever wondered where this internal experience comes
from, what determines its quality? Here is one possibility . . .

The way we are when we walk up to hit a golf shot, and

the way we are after we've hit the shot, has *nothing* to do with our past and everything to do with our relationship to the future. What I mean is that it's not the past that creates the present. How we are in the present moment is created by our relationship to our perceived future. This might sound bizarre, but hang in there with me and I'll explain.

As I mentioned in *Extraordinary Golf: The Art of the Possible* (my first book), I've asked thousands of golfers why they get upset when they mishit a shot. They say probably the same things you might say: "It didn't match my expectations," "I missed an opportunity," "I was embarrassed," "I failed," etc.

I've asked them to consider that none of these are the real source of their upset. Perhaps the only reason we get upset when we mishit a shot is because we *think we're going to do it again . . . in the future.*

For example, suppose you knew that on the first tee you were going to top the ball 20 yards, but you also knew that after that you would play the most magnificent round of your life. Would you be upset after that first shot? Every person to whom I've asked the question has answered no.

So a topped shot in the past, by itself, is not the source of the upset. But a topped shot coupled with a thought—a projection—seems to determine a golfer's state of mind. If the thought is some version of "this is going to continue," then there is upset. However, if the golfer somehow sees— and creates—that a wonderful future is possible, then there is no upset. Amazing!

So the source of the upset is clearly not from the incident itself (the topped shot) but from the way we perceive it. It's very powerful to realize that we're the ones creating the whole drama and that it has very little to do with the shot.

Let's keep going. Where do expectations, embarrassment, frustration and doubt come from? The past? The present? The future? Obviously they are historically based, from the past. So let's observe the entire mechanism of the upset. You top a shot. At that moment your mind goes into the past and recalls similar past events and projects those memories, *in that moment,* into a future (it will happen again). These past memories, now misplaced into the future (and believed to be the *real* future), create an upset. And the upset will last until we put something in the future that gives us new possibilities, ones other than endless repetition of an upsetting past.

So we either have the past in the future (which makes life predictable) or we put the past back in the past (where it belongs) and create a new future where anything is possible. Life therefore becomes either a predictable reaction to the past or an enlivening, created possibility. It's possible to walk up to the next shot with either frame of mind, but rarely do we realize we have the power to choose.

It's obvious that our relationship to the future has a lot to do with how we experience this present moment. If you knew that just after reading this section of the book you were going to eat your favorite meal, you'd be experiencing this moment in a particular way. Alternatively, if you knew that after reading this section you were going to have a much needed but dreaded conversation with a family member, your internal experience while reading would change significantly.

As we said earlier, the future resides in a conversation we're having with ourselves now. The past also resides in a conversation we're having with ourselves now. And finally, there's what's actually happening now, outside of those internal conversations—that's the present. The future and past happen in our mind and the present happens outside of our mind. All these are going on in the only moment that can ever be: now.

What kind of a picture of the future do you have? Where does it come from? My brother Pete once asked a group of fifth-graders to draw a picture of the future. The kids drew images filled with high-tech gadgets, tall metal buildings, flying cars, robots and transportation systems bringing thousands of identically dressed commuters to work. This was their picture of the future.

He then asked them what they most look forward to. They said being with their friends, going to the beach, vacationing with their family, playing sports, doing art. "Well," he asked, "if your pictures of the future were to become real, would you want to work and live there?" They answered, "Noooooooooo! It wouldn't be much fun."

I've asked many people how they view the future, and most have described scenarios filled with a great deal of anxiety, fear and resignation; ones in which they feel separated from, instead of connected to, others; ones filled with technology more than nature; ones with more work than they want; ones where they are doing what they think they must, rather than what they love. Why?

During the PGA Coaching & Teaching Summit, I noticed that not only was no one talking about a future of golf that turned all of us on, but no one was talking about a future at all! I began to ask many attending pros, "What do you say is the future of golf?" I know the power of that question because our actions today are always consistent with that future.

Their answers had a lot to do with technology, desire for increased numbers of players, a better economy and new ways to fix swings. These are very bright men and women who seemed accepting of a cultural future that is, they say, inevitable and unstoppable. When I asked them if this is the future they want, they answered no, but "that's the way it is."

Where does this picture come from, and how did it get embedded in these professionals?

I wanted to pause the proceedings and say, "We're the nucleus of the future of golf. We're the ones who can say how it goes. We can shift this culture. The only reason this 'other' uninspiring future is in place is because we keep it there. If we're the ones keeping it there, then we're the ones with the power to shift it. We are responsible for the future of golf—'responsible' as in 'we are able to respond, able to create.'"

We seem to be heading pell-mell toward a future in golf that no one really wants. It's not because of how society is, how people are, corporate influence or not enough energy/ time/money. We're heading that way because we haven't realized the immense power each of us has to create our own future.

Freedom, peace of mind and self-coaching won't happen on their own. A future that provides all three is not part of the automatic cultural future of right/wrong, good/bad swing and "our technology/economy will save us." A future of greater freedom, true peace of mind and greater capacity to self-coach will happen only if we create it—with each practice session, each round of golf, each conversation, each reverie.

The way we act at this moment is from a future that lives with us. That future is either given to us by our culture or personally generated. At any moment we are either holding someone else's future in place or creating our own. We are endowed with the power to generate either one.

Choose . . . or have it be chosen for you.

EPILOGUE

We human beings are truly amazing—at a deep level we are all geniuses. We've evolved through eons into these remarkable bodies, with amazing innate abilities. However, we require a certain type of environment to fully express these abilities. By "environment" I don't simply mean appropriate oxygen, temperature, food and sunlight. I'm also talking about an "internal" environment without evaluation or judgment, a place where it is safe to explore, a place where deep, rapid and complete learning can occur.

For fifteen years, Extraordinary Golf has intentionally created such an environment, one where students are acknowledged as fully capable, needing only to expand their awareness in order to develop. This unique environment has allowed for an honest exploration into learning, coaching and the nature of extraordinary development in golf. But for what purpose? This one:

Extraordinary Golf is committed to a future where golfers . . .

- experience the genius of their body and become advocates for others experiencing theirs;
- learn how to deal with the Voice in their heads and not have it stop them in golf or life;
- live in gratitude and appreciation more than hope and fear;
- create environments for themselves that are free from evaluation and judgment, where deep learning can take place;
- create competition as a healthy dynamic where the joy of overcoming obstacles is more important than winning, and the conversation about "what I learned" at the end of the round is the norm;
- learn to coach themselves, their mates and their kids in a way that empowers and builds self-reliance so that students see how great they are;
- realize that self-image is not derived from the flight of the ball;
- experience the real joy and adventure of learning;
- develop concentration and focus;
- discover extraordinary performance as a function of letting go, taking risks and rediscovering trust in our instincts;

- live with freedom, peace of mind and self-aware-
  ness that wouldn't have happened had they not
  stepped into the very heart and soul of the game.

And finally . . .

A future where golfers experience that hitting a piece of
rubber with a stick in a big park has added great richness to
human life.

APPENDIX

FLOW OF EXERCISES

We have a saying in Extraordinary Golf that goes as follows: "It takes a long time to get away from your instincts, but only a short time to get back to them." What this means is that even if you've had years of ineffective patterns, extraordinary breakthroughs are never far away. This outlook may seem overly optimistic, but it is backed by experience with thousands of students.

It's possible that any of these exercises can provide a breakthrough, and it's not necessary to do them in a specific sequence or to do them all. We have laid them out in what we feel is the most understandable and logical order, and it certainly makes sense to do them in this way, but don't feel that you have to. You may try them all and settle on a few favorites, and that's just fine. Remember, the exercises don't work—you do.

All the exercises are listed here for easy reference, in the same order as they appear in the book. For ease in finding the full descriptions and illustrations, each exercise has the page number of its location in the book.

• *The "Where Are You Now?" Exercise* • *(page 25)*

Putt for ten minutes in your normal way, simply observing what you do. Try to refrain from judging whether what you do is right or wrong; simply observe what's there. Pay particular attention to the following:

- what you tell yourself as you address the putt
- what tips you think you need to remember
- when judgments arise: before, during or after the putt

Notice how much you are "in" your head (thinking, remembering, judging, etc.). This exercise provides a baseline against which to measure how your performance, learning and enjoyment may change as a result of engaging in the following exercises.

• *Freedom Exploration Exercise #1a* •
The Spot (page 27)

(a) Place a golf ball on the ground. Kneel down and take some time to look at it and really see it. Look for the shading, the overall light and the sparkles. Look for what you haven't seen before.

(b) Keep looking at the ball for a few moments. Then, *without covering the top of the ball with your hand,* reach along the ground, hold the ball on the sides with finger and thumb and gently pull it away to the side *while keeping your eyes on the spot where the ball was.* As you look at the area where the ball was, what do you see? If you don't see anything, do it again. Take your time. Make sure you do not follow the ball with your eyes, but keep staring at the spot on the ground where the ball was.

• *Freedom Exploration Exercise #1b* •
The Spot While Putting (page 29)

Address a ball in your normal putting stance and, as before, look at the ball for a few seconds to let it fill your vision. Then putt the ball to no target and watch for the afterimage on the ground. See how long the spot lasts. Do this for ten minutes or so.

· *Freedom Exploration Exercise #1c* ·
The Spot to a Target (page 34)

Address a ball in your normal putting stance and, as before, look at the ball for a few moments to let it fill your vision. Then putt the ball to a hole and watch for the after-image on the ground. See how long the spot lasts. Do this for ten minutes or so. These "see the spot" exercises are about being present to a reality (a ball is real) rather than a story in your head. They're about letting go of interference, the mental chatter. Through these exercises you get an opportunity to see how good your body really is and to notice if the target takes you away from being present.

· *Freedom Exploration Exercise #2a* ·
The Flagstick (page 40)

Take the flagstick out of the hole and lay it about 6 inches to the side of the hole, extending left to right. (If you do not have a flagstick available use a long golf club such as a driver.) Stand about 6 feet away and putt at the flagstick stretched out on the green before you. Just putt with the purpose of hitting the stick. It doesn't matter where on the stick the ball hits. Putt a dozen balls and experience what your muscles feel like, where your attention is, how calm your mind is.

• *Freedom Exploration Exercise #2b* •
The Flagstick and the Target
(page 41)

Now turn and putt the ball to the hole—which should be about the same distance as the flagstick—and notice if anything is different. Pay attention to the tightness of your muscles, the freedom of your movement and the thoughts in your head. Go back and forth between putting to the hole and putting to the flagstick to highlight any differences.

• *Freedom Exploration Exercise #3a* •
Adding Numbers (page 47)

Address a ball about 4 feet from a hole. Have a partner crouch behind the hole, facing you. When you are ready to putt, turn your head to look at the hole, say "go" and putt, looking only at the hole. As soon as you say "go," your partner displays three numbers (from 1 to 5) at an even pace at the back of the hole. Add the numbers while putting and say the total. Once you turn your head and say "go," do not look back at the ball.

This exercise breaks up the myth of "If I think the right thoughts, I'll hit the ball better and make more putts." It promotes a sense of "other than mind," pointing us to our body's innate ability when a real connection to the target is established.

• *Freedom Exploration Exercise #3b* •
Looking at the Hole (page 51)

Address a ball about 4 feet from a hole. When you are ready to putt, turn your head to look at the hole and focus on an area at the back of the hole. Putt while keeping your eyes and focus there, and do not look back at the ball. The quality of your attention on the hole is what's important here.

Are you able to focus and be as fully engaged as you were while adding the numbers?

• *Freedom Exploration Exercise #3c* •
Connecting to the Target (page 52)

Address a ball about 4 feet from a hole. Turn your head to look at the hole and focus on an area at the back of the hole. Then look at the ball, keeping the sense of connection with the target, and putt. Notice if the connection to the target is similar to when you were looking at the hole.

Can you maintain the same sense of the target when you look at the ball? Can you stay connected to the target throughout the stroke even though your eyes are not on it?

• *Freedom Exploration Exercise #4a* •
Enjoying the Motion (page 65)

Make your normal putting motion and, without using a ball, notice if the motion feels enjoyable to you from beginning to end. Let go of the mechanics for now and simply notice how your body feels while making this putting stroke. If it isn't completely enjoyable, experiment until you find a motion that is. The goal is to find a putting motion that is so enjoyable you would do it for its own sake.

· *Freedom Exploration Exercise #4b* · *Enjoying the Motion with the Target* *(page 66)*

Take this motion out to the practice putting green or to the golf course and see if you have enough awareness to accurately determine whether you enjoy the stroke itself. You'll quickly realize how much attention is required to experience the physical motion until the end of the swing. The challenge of this exercise is to stay present to your body until the end, not to evaluate how you did in the shot or whether you exhibited sound mechanics. Stay conscious of your intention and motion.

When you're on the course, consider keeping a separate putting "enjoyment score" on your scorecard, with a range from 10 (high enjoyment of the stroke) to 1 (low enjoyment).

· *Freedom Exploration Exercise #5* · *Exposing Interference (page 68)*

Find a partner, then go to a putting green with a bucket of balls and set the bucket on the green a few feet in from the edge. It doesn't matter where the nearest hole is, since you won't be putting to a hole at first. Have your friend kneel down by the bucket while you take a putting stance a few feet away. Your partner should be able to take a ball out of the bucket and place it where you can putt it.

You, the putter, simply swing back and forth with a putting stroke at the same height above the ground as if you were striking a ball. Continue back and forth without stopping until you find that free, enjoyable stroke. Tell your partner when you've found it and keep swinging.

Your partner then takes a ball and either places it so you strike it (while you continue your ongoing motion like a pendulum) or fakes placing it on the ground and takes it back at the last moment. Your job, as the putter, is to continue without stopping. Your partner's job is to place balls periodically at a frequency that's unpredictable to you.

It's rare for us to experience how we interfere. The path to freedom in putting is not in avoiding the interference, or in pretending that it's an issue of technique, but rather in exposing the interference, bringing it out in the open.

• *Freedom Exploration Exercise #6a* • *Reaction Putting (page 74)*

Find a partner and stand on the green about 6 feet apart, facing each other. Your partner has a putter and you have a golf ball. Roll a ball at moderate speed to your partner and have him putt it back to you. The goal is not to hit any particular spot, just to hit the ball back in your general direction. Ask your partner to notice how his body feels, what tension exists, what part of his body is being used. Ask him to feel the pacing of the stroke. Roll the ball to him about twenty times, then switch so that you, too, can experience the exercise.

• *Freedom Exploration Exercise #6b* •
Reacting Putting to a Hole (page 76)

This is the same scenario as the previous exercise, with both people about 6 feet apart, except that the person rolling the ball is next to a hole. Have your partner roll a ball and putt it back to him as before. Notice the experience. Then instead of hitting the next ball right back to him, stop the ball with your putter, take a very short pause and then putt it back toward the hole. Notice if there is a difference between this experience and the previous one. Continue this pattern of first hitting a rolling ball, then stopping the ball, pausing and putting it toward the hole, noticing the differences. Gradually let the balls you stop rest for a longer time before you putt them. Then switch roles.

This exercise is intended to have us differentiate the experience of reacting spontaneously from that of calculating and manipulating.

• *Peace of Mind Exploration Exercise #1* •
The Voice (page 91)

Place a ball on the putting green one inch from a cup, address it in your normal way and putt it in. Notice if there is any doubt—any voice in your head. Repeat this several times, and use this experience as a baseline. Then move the ball away from the hole in 6-inch increments, putting it each time. Notice when the experience first begins to differ from the baseline, and what form this difference takes.

True peace of mind comes simply from letting go of that which disrupts it. The only thing that disrupts it is this quiet conversation. Your capacity to recognize this intrusive voice, let it be and come back to the task at hand—the one that you have created—is the training offered in this exercise.

• *Peace of Mind Exploration Exercise #2a* • *Concentration on the Clubhead* *(page 106)*

(a) Take your putter and assume your normal putting stance, but with no ball present. As you hold the putter, get a sense of the head of the club. Take a normal putting stroke and keep your attention on the clubhead, all the way from beginning to end. Notice if your attention shifts. Keep going until you feel your attention is consistently with the clubhead all the way through.

(b) Now do the same exercise but add a ball. Don't worry about putting to a hole or any other target. Simply address the ball, focusing your attention on the head of the club, and putt it, intending to keep your attention on the clubhead until the end of the stroke. Notice what happens, and if the presence of the ball affects your ability to hold your chosen focus.

• *Peace of Mind Exploration Exercise #2b* •
Deepening Concentration (page 108)

Do the same as in the previous exercise, picking one "real" part of the swing and staying with it through the entire stroke. Try this with your body, the ball or the target. As always, if your attention wanders, simply notice what it does and bring yourself back to your intended focus. It's likely that one of these areas of focus will prove to be the most interesting and enjoyable, and if so, stay with that. Remember that the goal is fascination, not hard work.

Two great sources of interference in golf are doubt and fear. When a person is present to what's here now (e.g., the clubhead), if only for the duration of the two seconds it takes to swing, there's no room for doubt and fear to come in. So being present to an area of the swing accomplishes two things: (1) you learn about the thing upon which you are focusing your attention, and (2) you leave no room for doubt, fear or other mental interference to come in. Exercises 2a and 2b address both.

• *Peace of Mind Exploration Exercise #3* •
Narrow Focus (page 111)

Take your sand wedge and go out to the putting green with a few balls. Stand 5 or 6 feet from a hole and putt the balls to the hole with the wedge. Notice what kind of focus it takes to hit the very center of the ball with the bottom edge of the blade. If you hit high, the ball will bounce. If you hit low, the ball will jump in the air. The challenge is to hit the ball so that it rolls smoothly to the hole.

Notice the sensitivity that's needed in your hands, and the kind of focus that is required. You may also find that the length and acceleration of your putting stroke change. Also note the relationship between concentration and peace of mind.

• *Peace of Mind Exploration Exercise #4* • *Exposing Judgments (page 116)*

Go to the putting green and simply putt balls to a target. Instead of watching the ball once you complete your stroke, watch the actual shadow that the ball makes (not the after-image) on the ground as it rolls. When the ball is touching the ground the shadow will be partial, but if the ball bounces you will see the whole oval shadow. Note what the experience is like when you're simply watching the shadow. We can call that "absence of judgment." Perhaps you're experiencing a state of mild interest or curiosity, or even amazement. Then alternate between watching the ball on a putt and watching the shadow on another putt. This exercise is to distinguish judgment from other states of being.

• *Self-Coaching Exploration Exercise #1* • *Reality Check (page 128)*

(a) With a partner (or a tripod), use a video camera (or a digital camera with video capability) to film your putting stroke from three perspectives: (1) from behind, full-body shot; (2) from behind, close-up; (3) from the side, full-body. Film several putts (about 20 feet) from each angle.

(b) Review the videos, looking not for what's wrong but for what surprises you—the things you didn't know were happening. Notice the difference between what you thought was the reality of your putting stroke versus what the camera reveals.

The purpose of this exercise is not to attempt to change the areas of your motion/setup you deem inefficient. Rather, it is to provide an opportunity to experience a blind spot, to become aware of something of which you were previously unaware. Attempting to change anything without experiencing it only ensures the persistence of the unwanted motion.

• *Self-Coaching Exploration Exercise #2* •
Reading Greens (page 139)

Go to the practice green and find putts that have varying amounts of break. Instead of putting, first simply roll balls toward the holes with your hand. Watch the entire length of the break. When you are aware of the quality of attention needed to see accurately, start putting and notice if the quality of your attention—your seeing—changes with the putter in hand.

This exercise is an opportunity to train yourself to see the break without the filter of expectation, judgment or hope.

• *Self-Coaching Exploration Exercise #3a* •
Is the Practice Stroke Enough? (page 144)

(a) Find a partner and go to the putting green with a supply of balls. Set up about 20 feet away from a hole and find a practice stroke you think is appropriate for that distance. Keep this same stroke continuously going back and forth, close enough to the ground that it would hit a ball solidly. Then close your eyes.

(b) Taking care not to touch your putter while it is moving, your partner occasionally places balls where the ball would normally lie. With your eyes closed, you will occasionally hit balls when they've been placed. Don't let the experience of ball impact stop you, just keep your eyes closed and keep the stroke going back and forth. (After a few ball placements, your partner will have found the spot to place the ball that allows you to hit it solidly, even with your eyes closed.) After hitting a dozen or so balls, open your eyes and notice whether the balls ended up where you thought they would.

• *Self-Coaching Exploration Exercise #3b* •
Interference in the Stroke (page 147)

(a) With the same partner and setup, take continuous practice strokes with eyes open until your partner determines that they are appropriate for the target (a hole about 20 feet away). Continue this same stroke and close your eyes.

(b) In the same way as before, your partner occasionally places balls for you to hit. After you hit a few, your partner tells you to open your eyes and places a ball down. Putt this last ball with eyes open and notice if there is any difference in your stroke. Repeat this sequence to highlight any changes caused by the presence of the ball.

This exercise is about finding out whether our practice stroke is appropriate to the target. If it isn't, our body seems to compensate (jabs, decelerates, etc.) when putting a ball. Since it is challenging for the body to calibrate the perfect amount of compensation each time, compensations usually yield inconsistent results. This process exposes our hidden compensations.

• *Self-Coaching Exploration Exercise #4a* • *The Blind Walk (page 154)*

(a) Go to a hole on the practice green and remove the flagstick. Also clear anything else from the vicinity of the hole and anything in your path. Stand approximately 20 feet from the hole and get into your putting stance. While you are in this putting stance, look at the hole as you would if you were to putt. Then, from that position, close your eyes and turn the putter upside down, holding the clubhead in your hand with the grip pointing downward (like a walking stick). Turn and start walking toward the hole with the intent to place the tip of the grip in the hole. Gently put the putter down where you think the cup is and then open your eyes. Notice where the hole is relative to where you thought it was.

(b) Repeat this sequence from different distances. Don't go back to the same starting point. Keep the distances longer than 10 feet for a while. Do not count your steps; do not use your memory. Just see if you can sense/perceive where the hole is. And begin to notice if there's a pattern. Do you tend to place the putter down short of the hole? Left? Right? Long?

• Self-Coaching Exploration Exercise #4b •
The Blind Walk—A Shift in Perception
(page 156)

Can you begin to see the hole as the middle of things? Can you begin to see the hole as part of a "whole"? Even while you are connected to the goal, can you stay connected to the wider vision? Start seeing the area in front of *and* behind the hole, so that the entire area around the hole becomes known and the hole becomes the middle of this known area. Take blind walks from different distances with this new way of looking.

Our putting stroke is a readout of how we see the green, much in the same way our actions are a function of the way we see the world. Instead of working on the putting stroke, this exercise works on how we see. See how seeing the hole in the middle of our known area changes both the walk and the putting stroke.

• Self-Coaching Exploration Exercise #5a •
Putt and Predict Direction (page 159)

Take the pin out of a hole and put a small cloth (a handkerchief or a washcloth) in the cup. Have the cloth line the cup in such a way that if the ball were to go in, the cloth would muffle the noise so you wouldn't hear it. Set up about 10 feet away, in a spot where you have a straight putt (no break). Putt balls from this distance with your eyes closed. Can you predict where the balls stop relative to the cup without seeing them? Then experiment with a variety of distances and curves (breaks). Don't open your eyes until well after the balls have stopped. Remember that it takes several seconds after you've hit a putt to process all the feedback. In the first part of the exercise, simply predict whether the balls end up left, right or straight at the hole.

• *Self-Coaching Exploration Exercise #5b* •
Putt and Predict Distance (page 160)

With the hole still muffled, place markers at one-foot increments in front of and behind the hole, and several feet to the side. Again putt balls with your eyes closed, this time guessing distance as well as line, using the markers as reference. Try to visualize the full path of the ball before you open your eyes. Can you sense not only where the ball ends up but also when and how it gets there?

You'll need to tune in to the putter face, your body and the target in order to predict accurately. It's possible to develop your senses to a point where you don't need a sound or a visual confirmation to tell you if the ball is in the hole. As your predictions grow in accuracy, so will your putts. It just happens: Awareness is developmental.

THE WORLD OF EXTRAORDINARY GOLF

Extraordinary Golf is headquartered in Carmel, California, and gives workshops there, in Palm Springs, California, and many other places around the country and globe. Extraordinary Golf is committed to providing an environment in which an unpredicated and unpredictable transformation is possible, in golf or in any endeavor.

The organization was founded in 1990 and now consists of coaches whose wide variety of personal and professional experience makes for a rich and multifaceted base of knowledge. In addition to golf expertise—collectively, hundreds of thousands of individual lessons and thousands of workshops—there is extensive experience in business development and personal and executive coaching.

Extraordinary Golf has given golf programs for thousands of

golfers, teaching professionals and hundreds of organizations, including the PGA and LPGA, not only in the United States but in Canada, Japan, Spain and Argentina.

Extraordinary Golf
P.O. Box 22731
Carmel, CA 93922
Tel.: 1-800-541-2444 or 1-831-625-1900
Fax: 1-831-625-1976
E-mail extragolf@aol.com
www.ExtraordinaryGolf.com